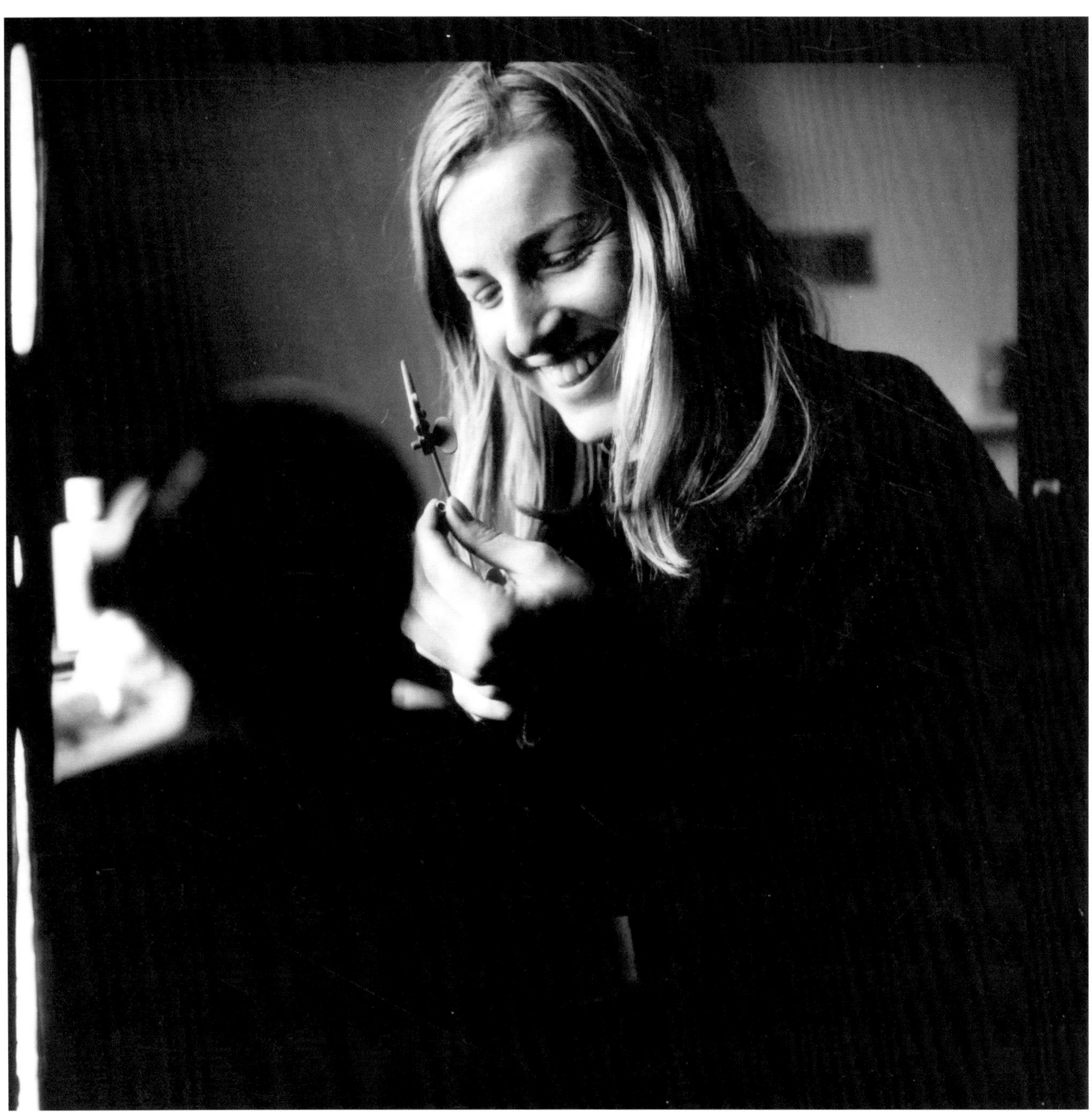

HELGA ZAHN

SCHMUCK. UNIKAT UND SERIE.
JEWELRY. ONE-OFF AND SERIES.

Mit einem Textbeitrag von Petra Hölscher
With an essay by Petra Hölscher

Kunstgalerie Altes Rathaus
Schwarzenbach a. d. Saale

Die Neue Sammlung – The Design Museum

Arnoldsche Art Publishers

Inhalt | Contents

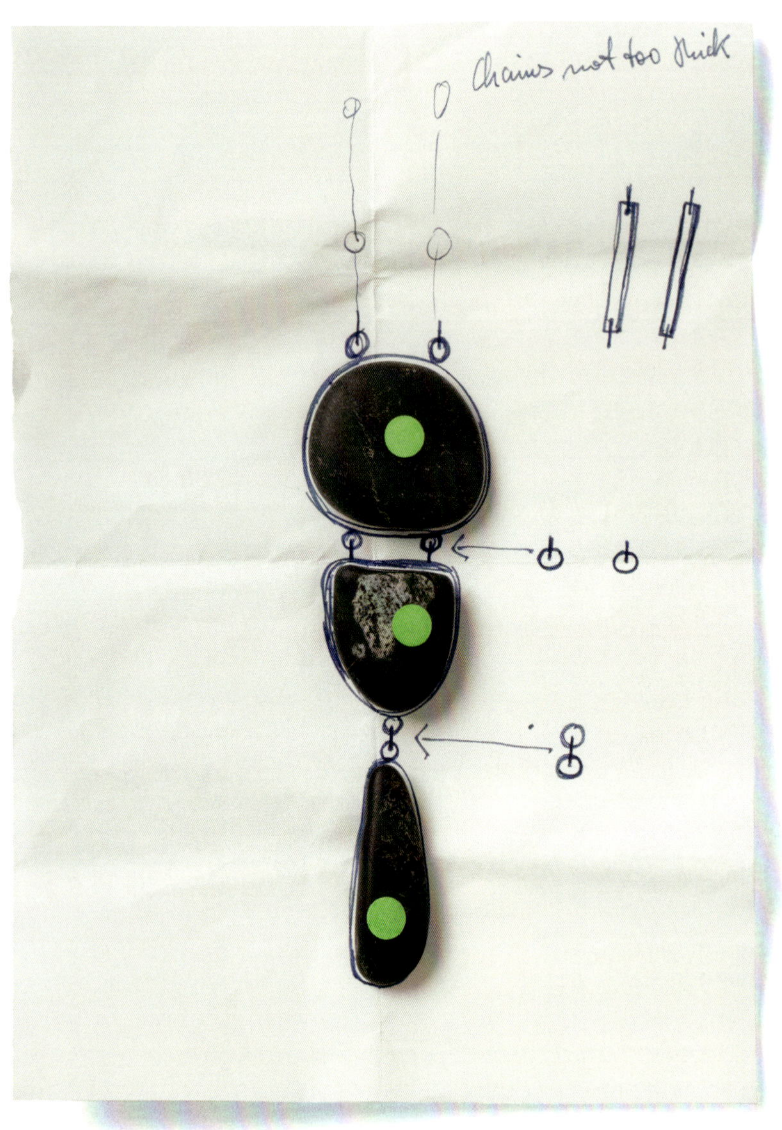

Entwurfszeichnung mit 3 Steinen für einen Halsschmuck
scetch with 3 pebble stones for a necklace, 1962
Papier, Kieselsteine | paper, pebble stones
H. 20,9 cm, B. 15 cm | h. 20,9 cm, w. 15 cm
Die Neue Sammlung – The Design Museum

Vorwort | Foreword

Helga Zahn – Schwarzenbacherin – Schmuckkünstlerin. Die einen kennen sie noch von Kindesbeinen an, erinnern sich an ihre Hippie-Kleidung und dass sie nach London ging, wo sie auch Schmuck gemacht haben soll … und die anderen bewundern ihre wenigen, in öffentlichen Institutionen zu sehenden Schmuckarbeiten. Man weiß nicht sehr viel über diese Frau, über diese vielfältig talentierte Künstlerin, die Ende der 1950er-Jahre aus Schwarzenbach an der Saale, einer kleinen Stadt am Rande des Fichtelgebirges, in das „Swinging London" ging und dort schon bald mit ihrem außergewöhnlichen Schmuck Furore machte.

Was lag näher, als sich gemeinsam – die Kunstgalerie Altes Rathaus der Stadt Schwarzenbach und Die Neue Sammlung in München und dankenswerter Weise auf Initiative der Dr. Hans Vießmann-Stiftung – auf den Weg zu machen, die Schmuckkünstlerin Helga Zahn zu entdecken. Oder besser gesagt: wieder zu entdecken für Schwarzenbach und für die Welt des Autorenschmucks.

Dabei war sie präsent in dieser speziellen Welt der schmückenden Artefakte, hatte man ihr doch 1966 für ihre einzigartigen, archaischen, mit Naturmaterialien gestalteten und so noch nie zuvor gesehenen Arbeiten die Goldmedaille des Bayerischen Staatspreises verliehen – zur damaligen Zeit für viele Künstler der Freifahrtschein zum Erfolg. Präsenz zeigte sie auch in Schwarzenbach, brachte ihre weltläufigen Freunde mit in ihre

Helga Zahn – from Schwarzenbach, studio jewelry artist. Some know her from their childhood days, remember her Hippie clothes, how she went to London, where she is said to have made jewelry among other things … and the others admire her few jewelry pieces on show in public institutes. Not much is known about this woman, about this multi-talented artist who at the end of the 1950s headed from Schwarzenbach an der Saale, a small town on the edge of the Fichtel Mountains, for "Swinging" London and very soon was causing a real stir with her extraordinary jewelry.

What seemed more obvious than to set out together to discover Helga Zahn the studio jewelry artist, with Schwarzenbach's Kunstgalerie Altes Rathaus and Munich's Die Neue Sammlung – and we are most grateful to the Dr. Hans Vießmann Foundation for taking the initiative. Or rather, to rediscover her work on behalf of Schwarzenbach and the world of studio jewelry.

She had a strong presence, after all, in that special world of decorative artifacts – back in 1966 she won nothing less than the Bavarian State Award Gold Medal for her quite unprecedented, unique, archaic works designed from natural materials – such an award was for many back then a carte blanche for success. She was also definitely present in Schwarzenbach, bringing her cosmopolitan friends back to her home town with her. Such as British Pop artist Peter Gee, who was based in America and not

Heimatstadt. Da war der in Amerika lebende britische Pop-Art-Künstler Peter Gee, der nicht nur 1970 in der Galerie Weinelt in Hof seine farbenfrohe Grafik ausstellte und dessen Arbeiten im Museum of Modern Art, New York, vertreten sind. Da war auch der heute als einer der wichtigsten portugiesischen Filmproduzenten geltende Eduardo Guedes, mit dem sie den Experimentalfilm „We Hope to Paint it Blue" realisierte, der 1970 im Central-Kino von Hof anlässlich der Eröffnung der Hofer Filmtage zu sehen war. Und da waren die Fotografin Tessa Grimshaw und ihr Bruder Nicholas, Architekt des Ludwig-Erhard-Hauses in Berlin, die Schwarzenbach gemeinsam mit Helga Zahn besuchten. Sie selbst war von 1969 bis 1972 vertreten auf den Ausstellungen der Schwarzenbacher Maler, sorgte mit ihren abstrakten, farbenreichen Siebdrucken für Aufsehen und zeigte ihren Schmuck in der Boutique Bijou in Hof.

Nun sind rund 100 Arbeiten Helga Zahns – Schmuck, Siebdrucke und Entwürfe – in einem Rückblick auf ihr künstlerisches Werk zu sehen. Dass dies in solchem Umfang möglich war, verdanken wir unseren zahlreichen Leihgebern, die alle mit großer Freude zum Gelingen der Ausstellung beigetragen haben – ihnen dafür unser ganz herzlicher Dank. Das Erspüren und Erforschen dieses facettenreichen Künstlerlebens, das uns nicht nur nach Schwarzenbach führt, sondern auch nach München, London und New York, wäre ohne die grandiose Hilfestellung der

only exhibited his colorful prints in 1970 in Galerie Weinelt in Hof – and whose works are included in the Museum of Modern Art, New York, collection. Such as Eduardo Guedes, today widely considered one of the most important Portuguese film producers, with whom she made the experimental film "We Hope to Paint it Blue", which was screened in 1970 in the Central-Kino in Hof on the occasion of the Hof Film Festival. Such as photographer Tessa Grimshaw and her brother Nicholas, the architect who designed the Ludwig Erhard Building in Berlin, and who visited Schwarzenbach together with Helga Zahn. She herself took part from 1969 to 1972 in exhibitions of Schwarzenbach painters, catching the eye with her abstract, colorful silkscreens, and presenting her jewelry in Boutique Bijou in Hof.

Now some 100 pieces by Helga Zahn, including jewelry, silkscreens and designs are on display as a retrospective of her artistic oeuvre. We have the countless persons who have loaned us works to thank for the fact that the exhibition has been possible on such a scale; they have all gladly contributed to the success of the show and we are most grateful to them. We would simply not have been able to track and research the truly multifaceted life of the artist, a project that takes us also to Munich, London and New York, without the marvelous help of the Zahn family.
As a result, we are proud to present the first scholarly outline of Helga Zahn's career. And last but not least we have the following to thank for finan-

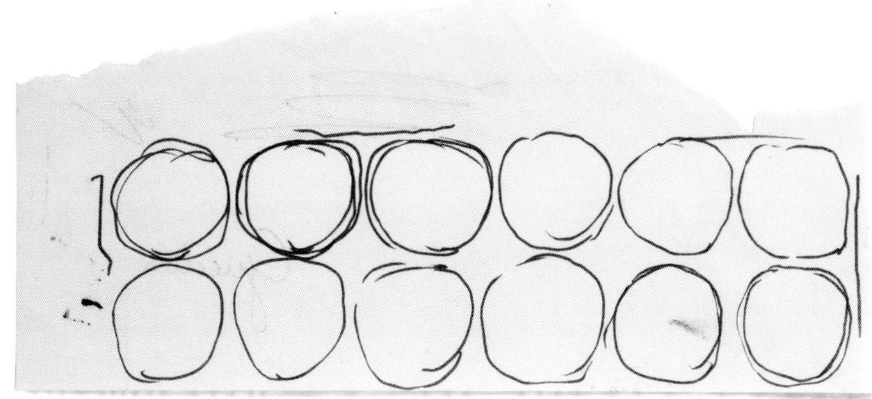

Entwurfszeichnung für einen Armschmuck
scetch for a bracelet, 1965
Papier, Filzstift | paper, felt pen
H. 9,5 cm, B. 20,3 cm | h. 9,5 cm, w. 20,3 cm
Die Neue Sammlung – The Design Museum

Familie Zahn ein nicht zu realisierendes Projekt geblieben. So liegt jetzt erstmals eine wissenschaftliche Aufarbeitung des Werdegangs von Helga Zahn vor. Schließlich blieb auch die Finanzierung von Ausstellung und Katalog dank der Christian-Heinrich-Sandler-Stiftung, der Danner-Stiftung München, dem Kulturverein Schwarzenbach, der Oberfrankenstiftung, der Gemeinnützigen Stiftung der Sparkasse Hochfranken und vor allem dank der Dr. Hans Vießmann-Stiftung nicht nur ein Wunschtraum. Die Realisierung von Ausstellung und Katalog wäre ohne den enthusiastischen Einsatz der Mitarbeiter der Stadt Schwarzenbach, hier vor allem von Barbara Muck und Sabine Oltsch, und den Mitarbeitern der Neuen Sammlung so nicht möglich gewesen – ihnen allen gebührt unser ganz herzlicher Dank.

Die Stadt Schwarzenbach freut sich sehr darüber, die Ausstellung anlässlich des 80. Geburtstages von Helga Zahn in der Kunstgalerie Altes Rathaus zu zeigen. Im Frühjahr 2019 wird Die Neue Sammlung die Werkschau für die Besucher und in ihrer seit 2006 jährlich stattfindenden Schmuckausstellung auch in der Pinakothek der Moderne in München öffnen – beide Ausstellungsorte schon früher wichtige Stationen im Leben von Helga Zahn.

Stadt Schwarzenbach a. d. Saale
Die Neue Sammlung – The Design Museum

cing the exhibition and the catalog: the Christian Heinrich Sandler Foundation, the Danner Foundation Munich, Kulturverein Schwarzenbach, the Oberfrankenstiftung, the Gemeinnützige Stiftung der Sparkasse Hochfranken and above all the Dr. Hans Vießmann Foundation for making a dream come true. The realization of both the exhibition and the catalog would not have been possible with such great results without the enthusiastic efforts of the staff of the Town of Schwarzenbach, above all Barbara Muck and Sabine Oltsch, and the staff at Neue Sammlung and we would like thank them all most cordially.

The Town of Schwarzenbach is delighted to present the exhibition on the occasion of the 80th birthday of Helga Zahn in Kunstgalerie Altes Rathaus. In spring 2019 Die Neue Sammlung will also host the exhibition – in the tradition of studio jewelry exhibitions since 2006 – at Pinakothek der Moderne in Munich; both venues marked important stages in Helga Zahn's life many years ago.

Town of Schwarzenbach a. d. Saale
Die Neue Sammlung – The Design Museum

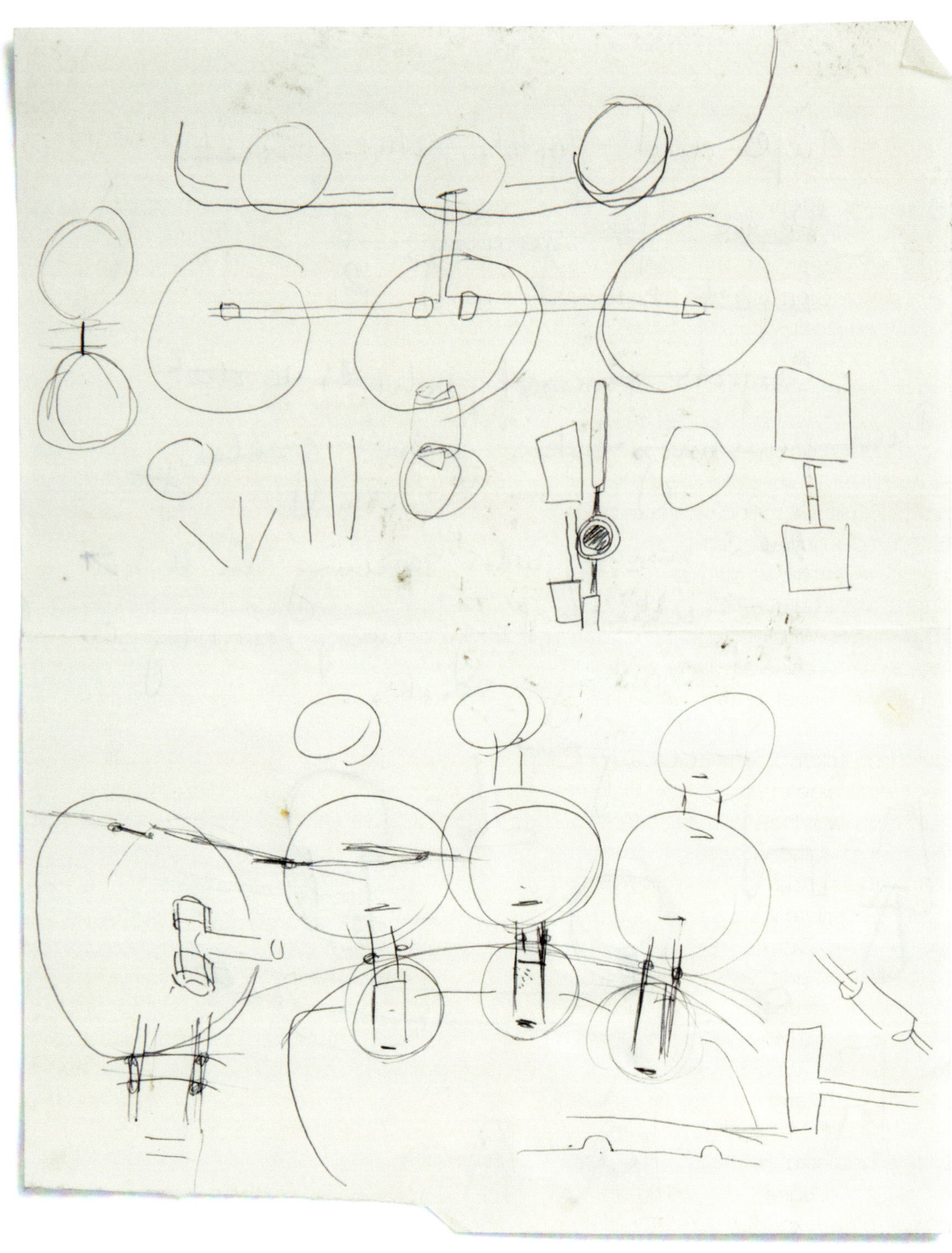

Entwürfe für einen Halsschmuck | scetches for a necklace, 1967
Papier, Kugelschreiber | paper, ballpoint pen
H. 25,3 cm, B. 20,3 cm | h. 25,3 cm, w. 20,3 cm
Die Neue Sammlung – The Design Museum

Helga Zahn

Schmuck. Ich liebe es, ihn zu machen, und zugleich hasse ich es.

Der kreative Prozess ist kurz, die Ausführung langwieriger und ermüdend.

Das Herstellen ist für mich eine Übung, ein Spiel mit Metallen, Werkzeugen, Steinen, Formen, Farben, Kompositionen, ihren Beziehungen zueinander, und im fertigen Produkt die dekorative Wirkung auf die menschliche Gestalt, den Körper.

Ich mache mir keine Gedanken darüber, wer ihn trägt, wer ihn kauft, wer ihn mag, ausstellt, verwendet oder überhaupt nicht mag.
Ich mache ihn.

Manchmal zeichne ich, manchmal kritzele ich, manchmal hinterlasse ich überhaupt keine schriftlichen Aufzeichnungen. Ich habe jedoch immer eine klare visuelle Empfindung der Qualität und der gesamten Wirkung, die ich erreichen will, vor mir. Qualität ist dasjenige, das ich beständig in einer Arbeit oder bei anderen Menschen suche.

Qualität wird im Lexikon definiert als „hervorragende Eigenschaft; eine ausgeprägte Eigenheit oder Merkmal; das, was Individualität vermittelt; ein geistiges oder moralisches Merkmal oder Charakteristikum; besondere Fähigkeit, Wert oder Funktion; besondere Wirksamkeit, hoher Leistungsgrad, relative Güte".

Handwerkliche Kunst und Gestaltung kommen erst an zweiter Stelle, sie unterliegen dem Wechsel von Geschmack und Mode, sind auf ihre jeweilige Zeit beschränkt. Wohingegen kreative Qualität über Jahrhunderte hinweg unbeschadet bleibt und von den Menschen, die ihr begegnen, gefühlt und erkannt wird.

Ich sollte vielleicht erklären, warum ich die Herstellung von Schmuckgegenständen auch hasse. Und ich hasse sie, nicht nur weil die eigentliche Schaffensperiode sehr kurz und der Herstellungsprozess sehr ermüdend ist, sondern wegen ihrer, dem Künstler auferlegten Beschränkungen sich auszudrücken; und auch wegen des

Jewellery. I love making and hate making.

The creative process is short, the execution long and tedious.

For me the making is an exercise, a play with metals, tools, stones, forms, colours, compositions, their relationship to each other and in the finished product the decorative effect to the human form, the body.

I do not worry about who may wear it, who may buy it, who may like it, exhibit it, use it, or totally dislike it.
I make it.

Sometimes I draw, sometimes I scribble, sometimes I leave no visual record behind at all.
I have, however, always a clear visual record behind feeling before me of the quality and total effect I am trying to achieve. Quality is the one thing I am constantly looking for in a piece of work and in other human beings.

Quality in the dictionary is defined as "distinguished character, a distinctive property or attribute, that which gives individuality; a mental or moral trait of characteristics; particular capacity, value, or function; particular efficacy, degree or excellence, relative goodness."

Craftsmanship and design come second, they are subject to tastes and fashions, limited to their time. Whereas creative quality will travel undisturbed across centuries and will be sensed and recognised, when people meet it.

I ought to explain why I also hate making jewellery. And I do, not only because of the process of making very tedious, but because of its limitations in self expression and materialistic overtone the word "jewellery" carries.

I tried once to break the rule with a brooch I made, with a quotation by Karl Marx inside it (p.92). The piece in itself is a contradiction too.

Compared to its creative quality, the whole concept of money making jewellery today is a contradiction and for me of total unimportance.

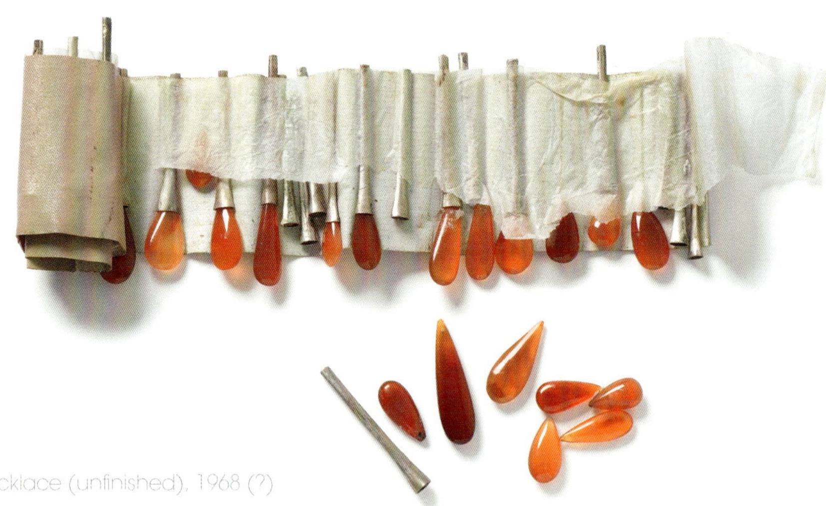

Halsschmuck (unvollendet) | necklace (unfinished), 1968 (?)
Silber, Bernstein | silver, amber
Privatbesitz | private property

materialistischen Obertons, den das Wort „Schmuck" mit sich trägt.

Einmal habe ich versucht, diese Regel mit einer Brosche zu durchbrechen, die innen ein Zitat von Karl Marx sehen lässt (S. 92). Das Stück ist in sich selbst ein Widerspruch, wie auch das Zitat (...).

Verglichen mit seiner kreativen Qualität ist das ganze heutige Konzept der Herstellung von Schmuckgegenständen um des Geldverdienens willen ein Widerspruch und von völliger Bedeutungslosigkeit für mich.

Text erstmals abgedruckt in | first published in: Ausst.-Kat. exh. cat. A Retrospective Assessment 1960–1976. Jewellery, Prints and Drawings. Crafts Advisory Committee, London 1976

"... Helga Zahn was an important liberating force in Britain in that time ... She often complained of the time-consuming process of goldsmithing and its debilitating effect on spontaneity, but she was never one to compromise, not least with the scale of her formidable work."

Ralph Turner, Kunsttheoretiker [1]

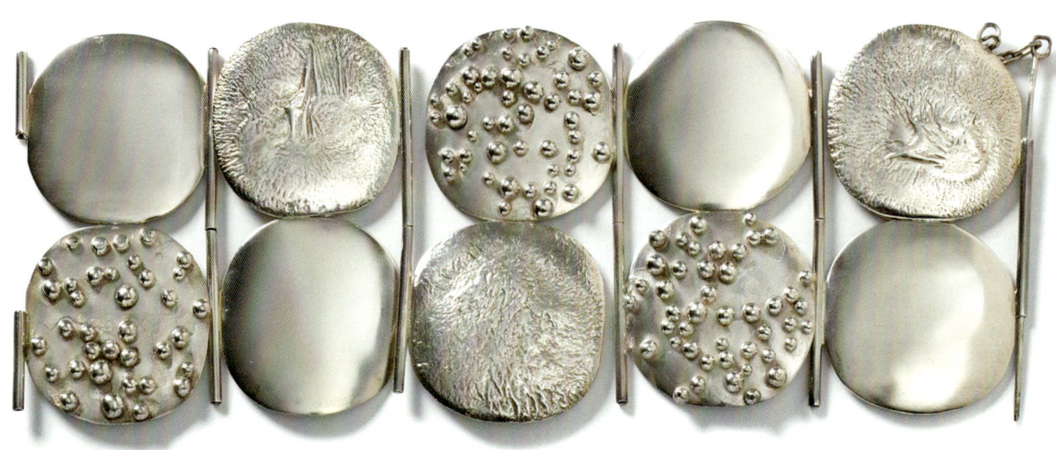

Armschmuck | bracelet, 1965
Silber | silver
H. 6,5 cm, B. 17,5 cm | h. 6,5 cm, w. 17,5 cm
Die Neue Sammlung – The Design Museum
Dauerleihgabe der Danner-Stiftung München
permanent loan of the Danner Foundation Munich

Petra Hölscher

Helga Zahn. Die Schmuckkünstlerin.

Helga Zahn. The Jewelry Artist.

München im Frühjahr 1966: Zum 17. Mal findet die Internationale Handwerksmesse statt. Als eine der wichtigsten nationalen wie internationalen Messen für Kunsthandwerk nach dem Zweiten Weltkrieg wird sie von dem damaligen Bundeskanzler Ludwig Erhard eröffnet. 18 Länder präsentieren in offiziellen Gruppenausstellungen das Kunsthandwerk ihres Landes, darunter auch Großbritannien. Es gibt eine Schmuckwerkstatt und eine Schmuckausstellung, die sich heute weltweit als eine der wichtigsten Ausstellungen für den so genannten Autorenschmuck etabliert hat. Am Ende haben 350.000 Besucher die Messe gesehen, auf der seit 1952 der Bayerische Staatspreis für außergewöhnliche Leistungen vergeben wird. In den Tageszeitungen liest man, dass „von den ausländischen Ausstellern mit dem Staatspreis ausgezeichnet wurde: (…) Helga Zahn, London, für Halsschmuck und Armband aus Silber" (S. 14).[2]
Vor ihr hatten 1957 Anton Frühauf aus dem italienischen Südtirol, 1959 Friedrich Becker aus Deutschland, 1963 Irena Brynner aus Amerika und Klaus Ulrich aus Deutschland, 1964 Anton Cepka aus der Tschechoslowakei, Mario Pinton aus Italien und Reinhold Reiling aus Deutschland, 1965 Bruno Martinazzi aus Italien und schließlich 1966 der Schweizer Max Fröhlich diesen Preis erhalten. Alle ihrer Profession nach ausgebildete Goldschmiede, die heute als Begründer der seinerzeit noch jungen Autorenschmuck-Bewegung gelten.

Helga Zahn ist weder Gold- noch Silberschmiedin, sie ist Autodidaktin.

Zu diesem Zeitpunkt lebt Helga Zahn seit rund zehn Jahren nicht mehr auf dem europäischen Festland, sondern hat ihren Lebensmittelpunkt auf die britische Insel verlegt. Und wie bei der amerikanischen Schmuckkünstlerin Irene Brynner wird sehr schnell in Vergessenheit geraten, dass Helga Zahn einst in München zu den Preisträgerinnen und Preisträgern gehörte.

Munich in spring 1966: The International Crafts Fair was being held for the 17th time. One of the most important national and international trade fairs for arts and crafts in the post-War period, it was duly opened by then German Chancellor Ludwig Erhard. A total of 18 countries presented the arts and crafts of their respective nations in official group shows, among them Great Britain. There was a jewelry workshop and a jewelry exhibition – today recognized worldwide as one of the most important shows of studio jewelry. By the time the gates finally closed, some 350,000 visitors had strolled around the trade fair, at which since 1952 the Bavarian State Award for Extraordinary Achievements had been bestowed. The dailies wrote that "among the foreign exhibitors the State Award was won by: (…) Helga Zahn, London, for silver necklace and bracelet" (p. 14) [2]. Before her, the State Award had gone to Anton Frühauf from Alto Adige in 1957, Germany's Friedrich Becker in 1959, American Irena Brynner and Germany's Klaus Ulrich in 1963, Czechoslovak Anton Cepka in 1964, along with Italy's Mario Pinton and Germany's Reinhold Reiling, to Italy's Bruno Martinazzi in 1965 and finally in 1966 to Switzerland's Max Fröhlich. All of them were by profession trained goldsmiths who are today considered to have founded what was then still the young movement of studio jewelry.

Helga Zahn was neither a trained goldsmith nor a trained silversmith – she was self-taught.

At this point in time, Helga Zahn had for some ten years no longer lived on the Continent, but had shifted the focus of her life to the British Isles. And as with US jewelry artist Irene Brynner it very swiftly got forgotten that Helga Zahn was once one of the award winners in Munich.

Ten years before the end of World War II, Helga Zahn grew up in Schwarzenbach an der Saale, a small town of a little over 7,000 inhabitants on the

Zehn Jahre vor Beendigung des Zweiten Weltkrieges wächst Helga Zahn in Schwarzenbach an der Saale auf, einer kleinen Stadt mit etwas über 7.000 Einwohnern am Rande des Fichtelgebirges, zwanzig Kilometer von der Grenze zur damaligen Tschechoslowakei entfernt. Es sind die Porzellan- und Textilindustrie, die dem Ort in den 50er- und 60er-Jahren seinen Wohlstand schenken. Ihre Eltern führen das Lebensmittelgeschäft am Ort. Für die künstlerischen Ambitionen eines heranwachsenden Teenagers bleibt nur wenig Raum. Und so arbeitet Helga Zahn nach dem Besuch der kaufmännischen Berufsschule im nahe gelegenen Hof erst einmal in einer Drogerie mit angeschlossenem Fotoatelier in Kronach. Den ersten Schritt zur Freiheit bedeutet 1956 ein Aufenthalt als „domestic help" in London. Am Ende wird die junge Deutsche in der englischen Metropole bleiben.

1958 lernt sie dort den heute als Pop-Art-Künstler bekannten Grafiker und Designer Peter Gee kennen und lieben. Er nimmt sie während eines Streiks der öffentlichen Verkehrsbetriebe als Anhalterin mit. Für Helga Zahn beginnt im „Swinging London" der frühen 60er-Jahre eine Zeit des Ausprobierens: Sie gehört zu den Teilnehmern von Gees Abendkurs „Basic Design" und besucht die führende Londoner Mannequin-Schule von Cherry Marshall in der Bond Street. Sie nimmt Unterricht bei Ernst Berk, dem Begründer des Modern Dance in England, und belegt einen Kunstkurs an einer Sommerschule in Oxfordshire. Durch das Modeln freundet sie sich mit der Still-Life-Fotografin Tessa Grimshaw an, der Schwester des britischen Architekten Nicholas Grimshaw. Dank Tessa lernt sie den Mode-Fotografen Sidney Pizan kennen, dessen Fotos u. a. dem Modemannequin Twiggy zu Weltruhm verhelfen. Beide – Grimshaw und Pizan – porträtieren die Schmuckarbeiten von Helga Zahn in einer neuen, so noch nicht gekannten Art und Weise. Erstmals entstehen im Sinne modernster Produktfotografie hochwertige Aufnahmen im Bereich des Autorenschmucks und der jungen Deutschen kommt dabei eine Vorreiterposition zu: „... sie scheute weder Zeit noch Mühe, um gute

edge of the Fichtel Mountains, 20 kilometers from the border to what was then Czechoslovakia. The town prospered in the 1950s and 1960s thanks to the porcelain and textile industries. Zahn's parents ran the local grocery shop. There was little scope for the teenager's artistic ambitions. Thus, after attending commercial vocational college Helga Zahn first worked in a drugstore with a photo studio attached to it – in Kronach. Her first step into the big wide world was a period spent as "domestic help" in London in 1956. In the end, the young German elected to stay in the British metropolis.

It was there that in 1958 she met and fell in love with graphic artist and designer Peter Gee, today renowned as a Pop Artist. He gave her a ride when she was thumbing a lift during a public transport strike. For Helga Zahn the "Swinging London" of the early 1960s marked a period of experimentation: She was one of the members of Gee's evening class in "Basic Design" and attended the leading London modeling school run by Cherry Marshall in Bond Street. She also took lessons from Ernest Berk, the founder of Modern Dance in England, and attended art classes at a summer school in Oxfordshire. While modeling she became friends with still-life photographer Tessa Grimshaw, sister of British architect Nicholas Grimshaw. Through Tessa, Helga met fashion photographer Sidney Pizan, whose photos, among others, helped fashion model Twiggy achieve world fame. Both Grimshaw and Pizan portrayed jewelry by Helga Zahn in a new, completely unprecedented way. For the very first time, high-grade images of studio jewelry were created in line with state-of-the-art product photography and the young German woman's works blazed the trail: "... she shied no time or effort to get good photos made of her works; in this regard she had a far more progressive approach than other jewelry artists in London at the time" (p. 50, 51).[3]

When her residence permit expired in 1958 her application for an academic permit was

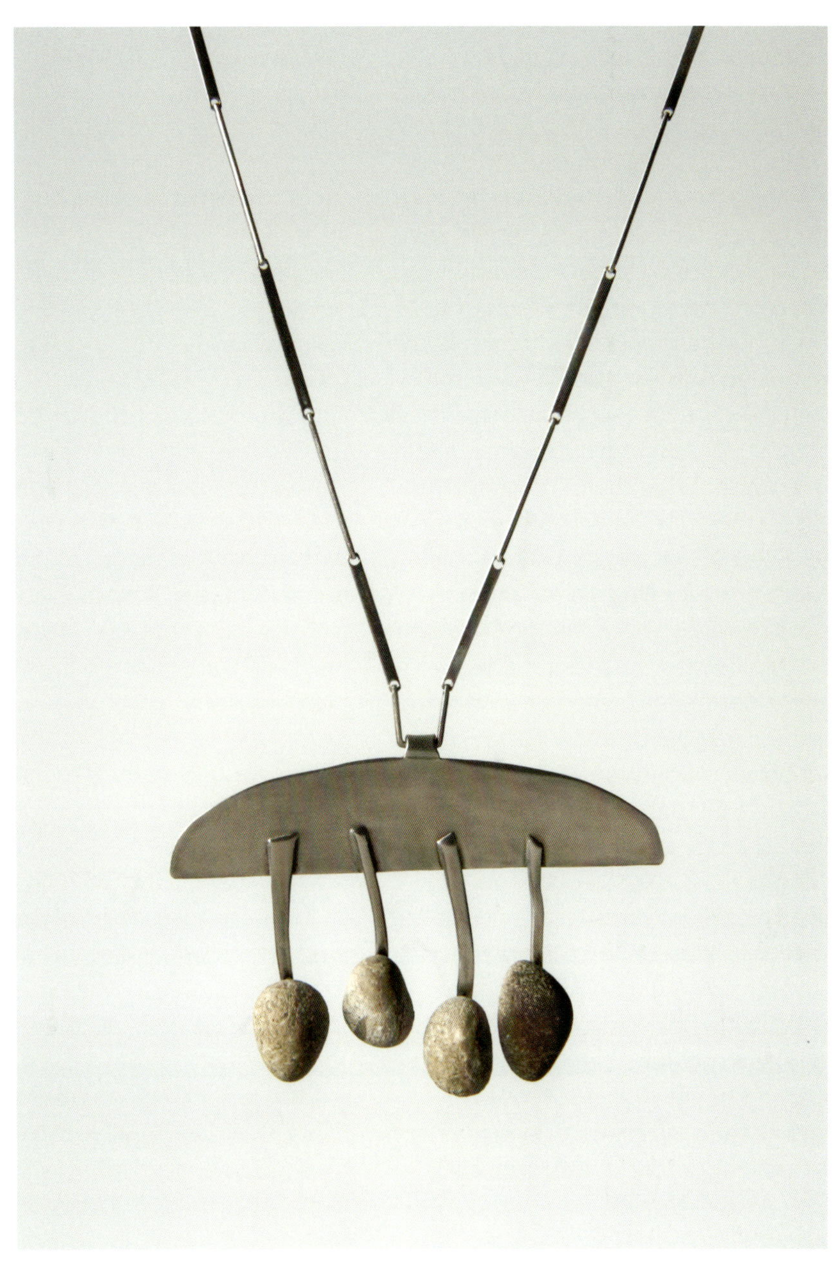

Halsschmuck | necklace, 1959
Silber, Kieselsteine | silver, pebble stones
H. 38 cm, B. 9,5 cm | h. 38 cm, w. 9,5 cm
Die Neue Sammlung – The Design Museum
Dauerleihgabe der Danner-Stiftung München
permanent loan of the Danner Foundation
Munich

Photo-Aufnahmen ihrer Arbeiten zu bekommen; diesbezüglich hatte sie weit fortschrittlichere Auffassungen als andere Schmuckkünstler im London jener Tage" (Seite 50, 51).[3]

Als ihre Aufenthaltsgenehmigung 1958 ausläuft, gibt man ihrem Antrag auf ein „Academic Permit" statt. Sie schreibt sich als Teilzeitstudentin für Kurse am Jewellery Department der Central School of Arts and Crafts in London ein (heute Central Saint Martins College of Art and Design). Hier entsteht eine ihrer frühesten bekannten Arbeiten aus dem Jahr 1959: ein Anhänger aus geschnittenem Silberblech mit aufgeklebten Kieselsteinen (S. 17). In seiner Radikalität jedweder Goldschmiede-Philosophie trotzend ist der Anhänger von einer außergewöhnlich archaischen Anmutung. Er stellt die bis dahin gültigen Schmuckkonventionen nicht nur der Londoner Bond Street, sondern auch von Goldschmieden und Künstlerkollegen auf den Prüfstand. Der künstlerisch hochwertige Entwurf mit unedleren Materialien unterliegt in seiner Wertschätzung nicht länger den materiellen Wertigkeiten von Gold, Platin und Diamanten. Und Helga Zahn beweist auf eindrucksvolle Weise, dass man keine ausgebildete Goldschmiedin sein muss, um qualitätvollen Schmuck zu entwerfen. Auch wenn sie in dieser Zeit ihren Eltern gegenüber den Wunsch äußert, an die Schmuckschule nach Pforzheim zu gehen, um ihrem bisher mit sicherem Instinkt umgesetzten ästhetischen Anspruch ein technisches Gerüst zu geben. Doch es bleibt ein unerfüllbarer Traum aufgrund ihrer finanziellen Lebenssituation.[4]

Gemeinsame Reisen mit ihrem Lebensgefährten Peter Gee führen Helga Zahn in den nächsten beiden Jahren immer wieder nach Paris, wo sie – neben Unterricht in Modern Dance bei Jerome Andrews – als freie Grafikerin erste Aufträge übernimmt. Es ist noch nicht entschieden, welche Passion die stärkere ist – Schmuck, Malerei oder Grafik. Mit Gee nimmt sie 1960 von Paris aus an einem Malerei-Sommerkurs von Victor Pasmore in Colchester teil. Zeitgenossen sehen in Pasmore den wichtigsten Vertreter Großbritanniens der „Real

approved. She enrolled as a part-time student for courses in the Jewellery Department of the Central School of Arts and Crafts in London (today's Central Saint Martins College of Art and Design). It was here that she created one of her first well-known pieces in 1959, namely a pendant made of cut sheet silver with pebbles glued to it (p. 17). In terms of radical thrust, defying all goldsmithing philosophies, it has an unusually archaic feel to it. It challenged the hitherto valid jewelry conventions not only on Bond Street, but also those of goldsmiths and fellow artists, too. High-grade artistic designs using less-precious materials were no longer to be appreciated only if they sparkled in gold, platinum and diamonds. And Helga Zahn proved emphatically that one did not need to be a trained goldsmith to design high-quality jewelry. Even if at the time she told her parents she would like to study at the jewelry college in Pforzheim in order to provide technical foundations for her aesthetic sense, which she had thus far applied with such a sure touch. Yet it was to remain an unfulfillable dream given the financial constraints she faced.[4]

Traveling together with her companion Peter Gee, over the next few years Helga Zahn repeatedly visited Paris, where in addition to studying Modern Dance under Jerome Andrews she landed her first contracts as a graphic designer. It was not yet clear which passion ran stronger, that for jewelry, for painting, or for graphics. Together with Gee in 1960 she headed from Paris to Colchester in the UK to attend a painting summer school run by Victor Pasmore. Contemporaries considered Pasmore the key champion of "Real Abstract Art" in Great Britain. Deeply impressed, Helga Zahn thereupon enrolled at the Leeds College of Art for the "Foundation, Form and Colour Studies" course developed by Victor Pasmore and Harry Thubron in line with Bauhaus ideals. The course enabled her thereafter to lecture from 1963 to 1965 at the College of Arts in Leicester, where she supported Tom Hudson in setting up the Foundation Studies program, akin

Abstract Art". Tief beeindruckt schreibt sich Helga Zahn daraufhin am Leeds College of Art für den von Victor Pasmore und Harry Thubron nach Bauhaus-Idealen entwickelten Studiengang „Foundation, Form and Coulour Studies" ein. Das Studium ermöglicht ihr im Anschluss daran von 1963 bis 1965 eine Lehrtätigkeit am College of Arts in Leicester anzunehmen, um dort Tom Hudson beim Aufbau seiner an Pasmore angelehnten Abteilung Foundation Studies zu unterstützen. Am College lernt sie den portugiesischen Filmstudenten Eduardo Guedes kennen. Er ist geflohen vor den Kolonialkriegs-Auseinandersetzungen in seinem Heimatland. Heute zählt man ihn zu den wichtigsten Filmproduzenten und -regisseuren Portugals.

Nur langsam stellt sich beim Schmuck der erhoffte Erfolg ein: Ein Kunstgeschäft in Central London hat ihren Schmuck in sein Portfolio aufgenommen und Helga Zahn ist das erste Mal von einer Galerie zu einer Gruppenausstellung eingeladen – der New End Gallery in London-Hampstead. Die Öffentlichkeit sieht in ihr spätestens jetzt eine erfolgreiche Jungkünstlerin, wie ein Interview im „Hampstead and Highgate Express" bestätigt.[5]

Mit diesem Erfolgserlebnis im Rücken reist Helga Zahn Weihnachten 1964 nach München. Sie besucht die Akademie der Bildenden Künste, die sie als „a very fine old building but extremely modern inside"[6] wahrnimmt. Ein Gespräch mit dem damaligen Leiter der Gold- und Silberschmiedeklasse, Franz Rickert, zieht sie aber dennoch nicht in Erwägung, zumal die Aufnahmebedingungen auch eine Ausbildung als Goldschmiedin vorgesehen hätten. Bei ihrem Spaziergang durch Schwabing, das sie mit dem Londoner Chelsea und Hampstead vergleicht, entdeckt sie „already a shop I would like to sell my jewellery in". Aber auch hier hat sie „no courage to talk to the owner".[7]

Stattdessen ergibt sich für Helga Zahn 1965 im Design Research Inc. in New York auf Betreiben von dem jetzt in Amerika lebenden Peter Gee die Möglichkeit einer ersten Einzelausstellung. In London kann sie sich an einer Gruppenausstellung in der noch jungen, aber viel beachteten Galerie

in approach to Pasmore's focus. There she met Portuguese film student Eduardo Guedes, who had fled the struggles in his native country relating to the colonial war. Today he is regarded as one of Portugal's most important film producers and directors.

Only slowly did her jewelry achieve the desired success: An art business in central London included her jewelry in its portfolio and Helga Zahn was for the first time invited by a gallery to participate in a group show – the New End Gallery in Hampstead. At the latest now the public came to see in her a successful young artist as was confirmed in an interview in the "Hampstead Highgate Express".[5]

With these successes under her belt, Helga Zahn traveled during the Christmas season 1964 to Munich. She visited the Akademie der Bildenden Künste, which she described as a "very fine old building but extremely modern inside".[6] Yet she did not opt for a meeting with Franz Rickert, the then Head of the Goldsmiths and Silversmiths Class, especially as admissions required having trained as a goldsmith. When strolling round the Schwabing quarter, which she compared to Chelsea and Hampstead, she discovered "already a shop I would like to sell my jewellery in," but here again she had "no courage to talk to the owner".[7]

Instead, with the support of Peter Gee, who now lived in America, in 1965 Helga Zahn had a solo show at Design Research Inc. in New York. In London she took part in a group show at the still young, but widely noted gallery of Ewan Phillips. It was the first gallery in London, if not in Europe, to include studio jewelry in its program.

The young art historian Ralph Turner worked here as an assistant. Only a few years later he joined forces with Barbara Cartlidge to open the first gallery devoted exclusively to young studio jewelry before moving on to the Crafts Advisory Committee. At Ewan Phillips' gallery, young British jewelry artist Wendy Ramshaw first encountered pieces by Helga Zahn and enthused "the items

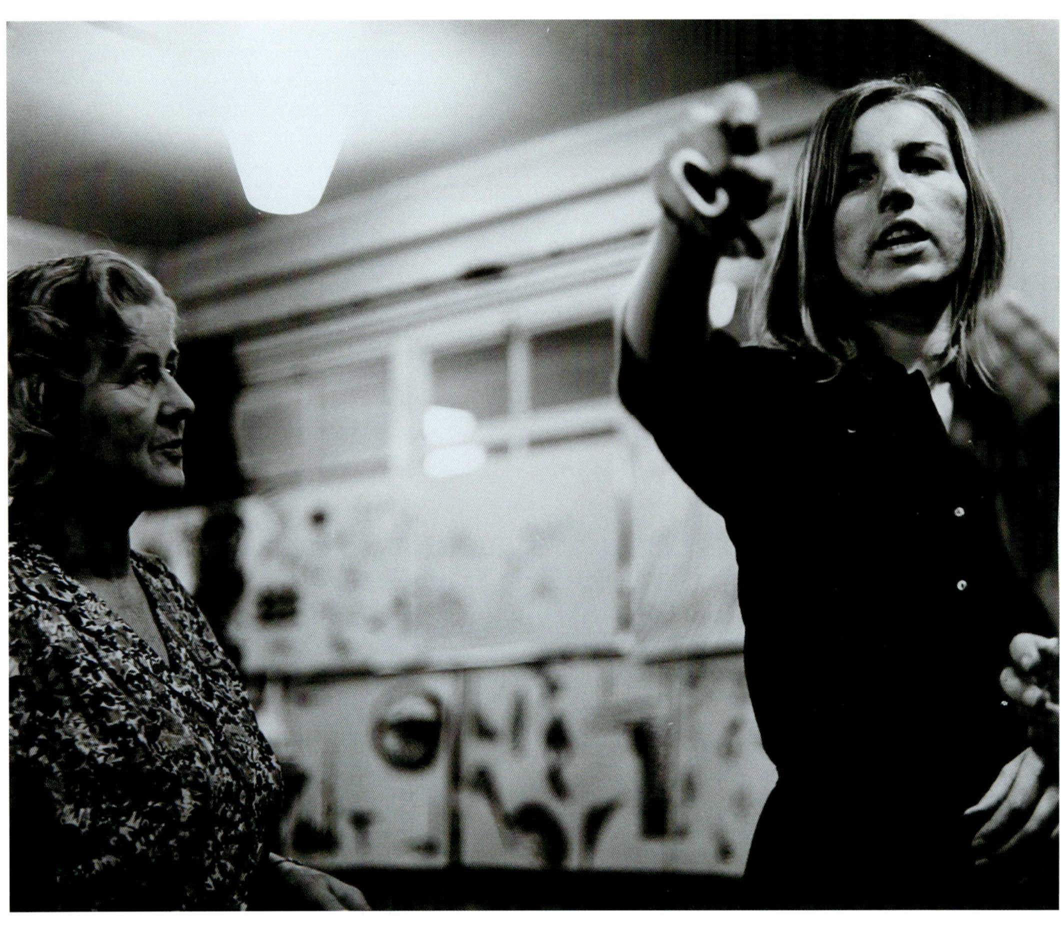

Helga Zahn 1963 in London
Foto: Archiv Helga Zahn

von Ewan Phillips beteiligen. Es ist die erste Galerie in London – eigentlich müsste man in Europa sagen –, die Autorenschmuck in ihr Programm aufnimmt.

Als Praktikant arbeitet hier der junge Kunsthistoriker Ralph Turner. Wenige Jahre später eröffnet er mit Barbara Cartlidge die erste Galerie, die sich ausschließlich dieser jungen Schmuckkunst widmet, bevor er dann an das Crafts Advisory Committee wechselt. Bei Ewan Phillips sieht die junge britische Schmuckkünstlerin Wendy Ramshaw erstmals Arbeiten von Helga Zahn und ist begeistert: „Die Schmuckstücke waren in der kleinen Galerie zusammen mit Arbeiten anderer Künstler ausgestellt, die ebenso Ideen für zeitgemäße Schmuckkunst auf neuen unkonventionellen Wegen entwickelten. Hervorstechend unter den ganzen ausgestellten Arbeiten war eine Kollektion mit großem Hals- schmuck und Ringen von Helga Zahn. Ihre Designs brachten starke, klare und positive Aussagen in den Exponaten zur Geltung."[8] Zahns Formensprache orientiert sich an den Umrissen der unpolierten und ungeschliffenen Kieselsteine. Es sind meist schwarze Steine, die sie in Cornwall findet. Die Fassung besteht dabei aus einem dünnen Silberstreifen, der sich um den Stein schmiegt (S. 64, 65). Bei anderen Stücken arbeitet sie die Steine als Solitäre in geschnittene Silberbleche ein, gehalten durch den jetzt aufgelöteten Silberstreifen. Bei stärker gerundeten Steinen schneidet sie auf der Rückseite ein Loch in das Silberblech. Aus dieser Vorgehensweise heraus entwickelt sie ein neues Gestaltungselement, indem sie die Rückseite zur Vorderseite erklärt (S. 23).

Mitte der 60er-Jahre, die ersten erfolgreichen Verkäufe sind zu vermelden, arbeitet Helga Zahn erstmals mit Materialien wie Perlmutt, Achat und Onyx oder archäologischen Artefakten. Dann bestimmen meist große runde und rechteckige Halbedelsteinscheiben die Entwürfe (S. 67). Zum Kauf der Halbedelsteine dienen Helga Zahn die Aufenthalte in der Heimat, um Kontakte nach Idar-Oberstein – etwa zur Firma H. W. Cullmann in Mörschied – oder nach Pforzheim zu nutzen, wo

of jewelry were on display in a small gallery together with works by other artists who likewise developed ideas for contemporary artistic jewelry along new, unconventional paths. What stood out from all the works on show was a collection of large necklaces and rings by Helga Zahn. Her designs made strong, clear and positive statements among the exhibits."[8] Zahn's formal language took its cue from the outlines of unpolished and unworked pebbles. Usually she chose black stones she had found in Cornwall. The settings consisted of a thin strip of silver into which the stone nestled (p. 64, 65). In other pieces she inset a single stone in cut sheet silver, held now by soldered silver strips. For more rounded stones she cut a hole in the back of the sheet silver. This approach led to a new design element evolving, as she made the reverse the front (p. 23).

In the mid-1960s, having made her first successful sales, Helga Zahn for the first time started working with materials such as mother-of-pearl, agate and onyx, as well as archaeological artifacts. Now, large round and rectangular semiprecious stones started to define her designs (p. 67). In order to buy the semi-precious stones Helga Zahn traveled home, where she relied on contacts in Idar-Oberstein (e.g., the firm H. W. Cullmann in Mörschied) or in Pforzheim, where a friend, jewelry artist Gerhard Huber, lived. Huber helped Helga Zahn in 1966 not only by providing advice on her own pieces, but also when designing and assembling the Christmas show at the Crafts Centrum in Bond Street.

Alongside her work with jewelry, Helga Zahn became a sought-after lecturer on painting and prints. From 1963 onwards she was permitted to lecture in Great Britain and from 1965, after teaching in Leicester, took charge of a summer course at Coventry Art College, where Robert Hedley Lewis was director. She taught at the Fine Arts Department of the City Literary Institute in London, where James Burr was at the helm, and her former place of study, the Leeds College of Art, tried to work her into a lectureship there (p. 20).

mit Gerhard Huber ein befreundeter Schmuckkünstler lebt. Huber hilft Helga Zahn 1966 nicht nur bei ihren eigenen Schmuckarbeiten mit Rat und Tat, sondern auch bei der Gestaltung und dem Aufbau der Weihnachtsausstellung des Crafts Centrum in der Londoner Bond Street.

Neben der Arbeit im Schmuck wird Helga Zahn zu einer gefragten Lehrkraft im Bereich Malerei und Grafik. Seit 1963 besitzt sie die Lehrerlaubnis für Großbritannien und übernimmt 1965 im Anschluss an ihre Lehrtätigkeit in Leicester die Leitung eines Sommerkurses am Coventry Art College bei Robert Hedley Lewis; sie lehrt am Fine Arts Department des City Literary Institute in London, das James Burr leitet, und ihre frühere Ausbildungsstätte, das Leeds College of Art, umwirbt sie als Lehrerin (S. 20). Sie entscheidet sich jedoch für die Lehrtätigkeit an der New Yorker Basic Research Unit Summer School von Peter Gee, die dieser gemeinsam mit Thomas M. Messmer, dem Direktor des Guggenheim Museums, als einen „experimental foundation workshop" entwickelt hat. Die Lehrtätigkeit ermöglicht ihr zugleich den Zugang zu den Schulwerkstätten und den Austausch mit den Werkstattleitern, sodass die Lehrtätigkeit aus vielerlei Gründen eine Win-win-Situation für sie ist.

1966 wird das bis dahin erfolgreichste Jahr für Helga Zahn. Im Frühjahr gelingt ihr die zu Beginn bereits erwähnte Teilnahme an der Internationalen Handwerksmesse in München, die mit dem Gewinn der Goldmedaille des Bayerischen Staatspreises für einen Hals- und Armschmuck gekrönt wird. Charakteristisch für ihren Entwurfs- und Herstellungsprozess ist schon hier das Arbeiten mit Schablonen. Nach einer ersten, oft flüchtigen Ideenskizze (S. 9) überträgt Helga Zahn diese 1:1 auf dünnes Zeichenpapier, um sie dann auf silberfarbenem, dünnem Karton durchzuzeichnen und auszuschneiden. Mit Hilfe der Kartonausschnitte kann sie das Schmuckstück auf vielfache Art zusammenstellen und seine Dimensionen überprüfen. Die auf das Metallblech gelegten Schablonen ermöglichen das leichte Ausschneiden der Form, das „in Silber oder Gold gemacht werden"[9] kann.

However, she chose instead to teach at the New York Basic Research Unit Summer School led by Peter Gee, who had set it up together with Thomas M. Messmer, director of the Guggenheim Museum, as an "experimental foundation workshop". Teaching also gave her access to the college workshops and enabled her to consult those running the workshops with all the technical questions, meaning teaching was a win-win situation for her at many different levels.

1966 was the most successful year hitherto for Helga Zahn. In the spring, as mentioned above, she took part in Munich's International Crafts Fair, and this was crowned by winning the Bavarian State Award Gold Medal for a necklace and bracelet. Characteristic of her creative and production method was her reliance on stencils. After a first, often fleeting sketch of the idea (p. 9) Helga Zahn transferred it 1:1 onto thin drawing paper before tracing the design onto thin silver-colored card and cutting it out. The cut-out card then enabled her to assemble the piece of jewelry in many ways and assess its dimensions. The stencil could then be placed on the sheet metal to simply cut out the shape, which "can be made in silver or gold".[9] The lack of accuracy in the cut-out silver blank is assumed as a given and/or given an artistic status, the edges bent inwards over a piece of wood and then cleaned up. In the case of the necklace that won gold in Munich, Helga Zahn left the surface smooth on some of the silver disks, on others she transformed it using a Bunsen burner and onto yet others she soldered tiny silver balls. Arranged in two rows, one above the other, and soldered onto a silver wire or held together by snap fasteners it was possible to assemble the silver disks in myriad combinations (p. 14, 39, 52, 53). Due to her lack of specialized knowledge, self-taught Helga Zahn developed a highly efficient technique using stencils in the mid-1960s. The concept of systematization is intrinsic to this technique; it even approaches a "democratization of jewelry". Ideally the cutting stencils in the corresponding

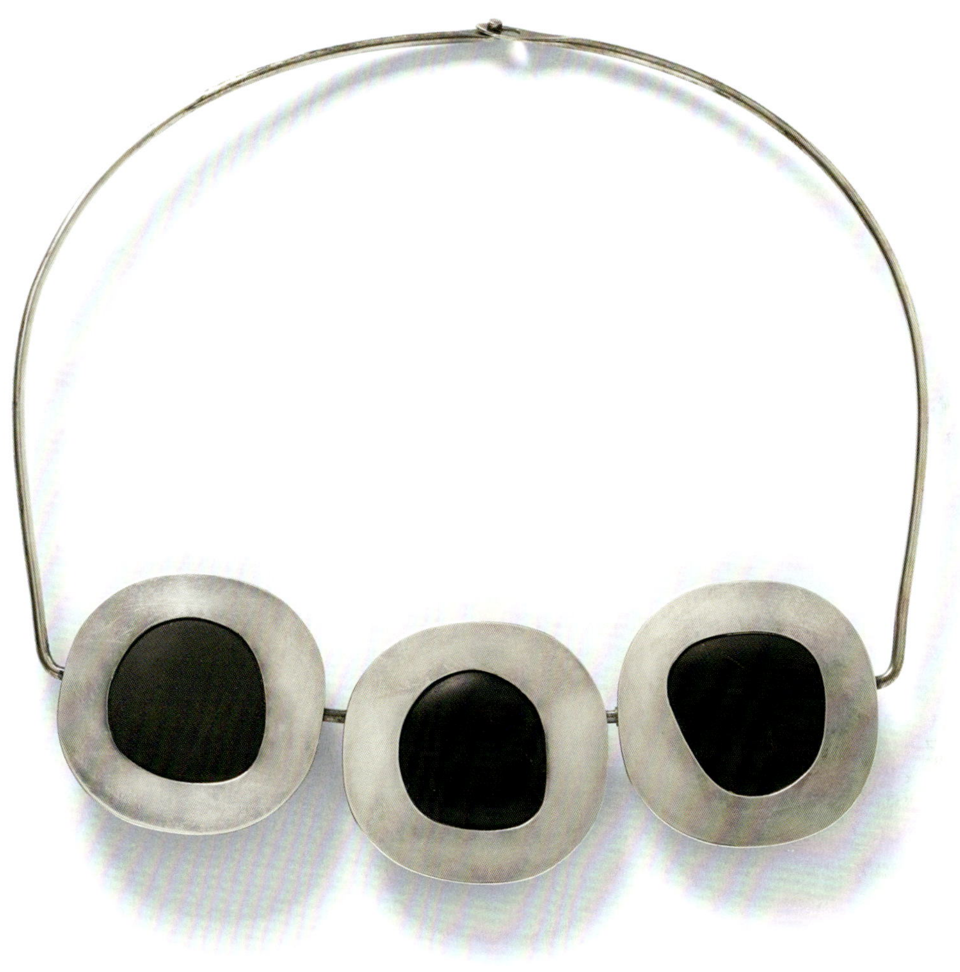

Halsschmuck | necklace, 1966/1967
Silber, Kieselsteine | silver, pebble stones
H. 18,3 cm, B. 19,3 cm | h. 18,3 cm, w. 19,3 cm
Privatsammlung | private collection

smiths Company in London offiziell als Schmuckmacherin eintragen. Die Punze trägt ihre Namensinitialen „HZ".

1967 hält sich Helga Zahn hauptsächlich in Nordamerika auf. Gleich zu Beginn des Jahres werden ihre Arbeiten auf einer Fashion Show des angesagten Modedesigners Tzaims Luksus gezeigt. Voller Stolz berichtet sie nach Hause, er habe „extra drei Kleider entworfen für meinen Schmuck"[10]. Sie übernimmt die Leitung eines Sommerkurses an der Haystack School of Arts in Maine und im Studio von Peter Gee kann sie ihre ersten Siebdrucke mit den Titeln „Effloration" – „Extemporisation" – „Extrication" – „Elucidation" – „Interpenetration" in einer Kleinauflage von 50 Stück drucken. Für die auf Holzplatten aufgezogenen Siebdrucke verwendet sie Rahmen aus starken Aluminiumleisten, die Robert Kulicke 1956 entwickelte und die bald darauf das Museum of Modern Art in New York als Standard einführte. Kulicke selbst gründet 1974 in New York eine Academy for Jewelry Art, an der Helga Zahn Ende der 70er-Jahre Kurse belegen wird.

Weniger erfolgreich verlaufen Zahns Versuche, auch 1967 und im darauf folgenden Jahr in München vertreten zu sein. Sind es erst organisatorische Gründe, ist es 1968 der verantwortliche Ausstellungsmacher Herbert Hofmann, der ihre Arbeiten zu zeigen ablehnt: „Leider aber wurde ich sehr enttäuscht, denn die beiden großen Stücke mit dem grünen, perlmutt und schwarzen Steinen wurden nicht ausgestellt. Herr Dr. Hofmann ist sehr, leider, conservativ."[11] Nach dieser Enttäuschung wird sie sich nicht wieder für die Schmuckausstellung in München bewerben. Aber sie gehört 1968 zu den Ausstellern der Internationalen Schmuckausstellung im damaligen tschechoslowakischen Jablonec. Die in Nordböhmen gelegene Kleinstadt, seit Mitte des 19. Jahrhunderts berühmt für ihre Modeschmuck-Industrie, richtet zum zweiten Mal nach 1965 eine internationale Schmuckausstellung aus. An der Ausstellung nehmen teil u. a. die Niederländer Gijs Bakker und Emmy van Leersum, die Engländer Wendy Ramshaw und David Watkins, die deutschen Professoren Reinhold Reiling und Fried-

Zahn's efforts to obtain representation in Munich in 1967 and the following year were less successful. Whereas at first organizational reasons were cited, it was the curator Herbert Hofmann responsible for the exhibition in 1968 who decided to reject her works: "Sadly I was bitterly disappointed, as the two large pieces with the green, mother-of-pearl and black stones were not shown. Dr. Hofmann is, unfortunately, very conservative."[11] Following this disappointment she did not reapply to exhibit at the jewelry show in Munich. But in 1968 she was among the exhibitors at the International Jewelry Exhibition in Jablonec in what was then Czechoslovakia. The small town in North Bohemia, famous for its fashion jewelry industry since the mid-19th century, staged an International Jewelry Exhibition for the second time in 1965. Dutch designers Gijs Bakker and Emmy van Leersum, British jewelry artists Wendy Ramshaw and David Watkins, the German professors Reinhold Reiling and Friedrich Becker, as well as the Italian artist Lucio Fontana took part in the exhibition, among others. The show provided the context for the first International Silver Jewelry Symposium Jablonec '68, featuring participants from both Eastern and Western Europe. The exhibition and symposium served to foster the Bohemian jewelry industry. Helga Zahn showed the necklace that had won her the prize in Munich. It was promptly featured in the East German trade journal "Uhren und Schmuck", but her name was not mentioned.[12]

Official graphic art commissions now also started rolling in. Felix Giacomoni, director of the Théâtre des Nations in Paris, appointed Helga Zahn to design the annual program of 1969 and a poster. Fritz Falk, director of the Schmuckmuseum founded in Pforzheim in 1961, showed her Pop Art silk-screen prints in a presentation at the Reuchlinhaus officially hosted by an organization going by the name of "Gruppe Junge Generation im Kunst- und Kunstgewerbeverein e.V.".[13] A small brochure designed by Helga Zahn and featuring an art print as an inlay was published in

rich Becker wie auch der italienische Künstler Lucio Fontana. Die Ausstellung bildet die Folie für das zum ersten Mal und unter Beteiligung von West- und Osteuropa stattfindende Internationale Silberschmuck-Symposium Jablonec '68. Ausstellung und Symposium dienen der Förderung der böhmischen Schmuckindustrie. Helga Zahn zeigt in Jablonec ihren zuvor in München prämierten Halsschmuck, der sogar in der ostdeutschen Fachzeitschrift „Uhren und Schmuck" abgedruckt wird, wenngleich ihr Name nicht genannt wird.[12]

Offizielle Aufträge stellen sich jetzt auch im Bereich der Grafik ein. Felix Giacomoni, Direktor des Théâtre des Nations in Paris, beauftragt Helga Zahn mit der Gestaltung des Jahresprogramms von 1969 und einem Plakatentwurf. Fritz Falk, Direktor des 1961 gegründeten Schmuckmuseums in Pforzheim, zeigt ihre ganz der Pop-Art verpflichteten Siebdrucke, offiziell firmiert die „Gruppe Junge Generation im Kunst- und Kunstgewerbeverein e.V." im Reuchlinhaus als Ausrichter.[13] Zur Ausstellung erscheint eine kleine, von Helga Zahn gestaltete Broschüre mit einem eingeklebten Kunstdruck. Das Begleitwort schreibt der in den USA und in Europa als Ausstellungskurator angesehene Kunsthistoriker Gene Baro. Bei dieser Gelegenheit erwirbt Falk eine Variante des in München hochdekorierten Halsschmuckes. Bedingt durch ihre vorherrschend schwierige finanzielle Situation, versucht Helga Zahn durch die Verwendung neuartiger Materialien neue Strategien bei ihrem Schmuck zu entwickeln. Gemeinsam mit ihrem Lebensgefährten, Eduardo Guedes, entwickelt sie Schmuck aus Nylon,[14] „um schnell, billig viel Geld zu machen, machen wir billigen, einfachen, gekünstelten Schmuck".[15]

In dieser Zeit reiht sich Ausstellung an Ausstellung für Helga Zahn: seien es nur die hier benannten Einzelausstellungen 1969 im ApoGee Studio, New York, und in der Nicholas Treadwell Gallery, London, gefolgt 1970 von Einzelausstellungen in der Gallery Richard Foncke im belgischen Gent oder in der Galerie Weinelt im oberfränkischen Hof. Gleichzeitig arbeitet Helga Zahn mit Eduardo

connection with the exhibition. The accompanying text was written by prominent exhibition curator and art historian Gene Baro, who was noted in both the US and Europe. Falk took this occasion to acquire an other version of the highly decorated necklace. Due to her prevailing difficult financial situation, Helga Zahn tried to develop new strategies for her jewelry practice by employing new materials. Together with her partner Eduardo Guedes she created jewelry using nylon:[14] "in order to make a lot of fast and cheap money, we are making cheap, simple, artificial jewellery".[15]

For Helga Zahn, one exhibition followed the other during this time. Even just in terms of solo exhibitions, she was extremely busy, showing at ApoGee Studio, New York, and Nicholas Treadwell Gallery, London in 1969, followed in 1970 by solo presentations at Gallery Richard Foncke in Ghent and at Galerie Weinelt in Hof, Bavaria. At the same time, Helga Zahn was working on a 20-minute experimental film together with Eduardo Guedes. "We Hope to Paint it Blue" premiered at the opening event of the 4th Hofer Filmtage film festival in 1970, at the Central-Kino in Hof. From 1969 onwards she was moreover a guest exhibitor at the annual "Schwarzenbacher Maler" shows, establishing her reputation with the "most discussed paintings"[16] there: "Top of the class with her screen prints (...) she creates formally rigorous compositions with circles and eccentrics in feminine Pop Art hues."[17] Visiting her home region led her to consider holding summer courses in painting, graphics and jewelry in Schwarzenbach, in order to help finance her stays there.[18] Yet this plan did not come to fruition.

In 1970 Fritz Falk invited her to take part in his survey exhibition "Schmuck 70 – Tendenzen". The second photo no less in the category "Individually designed gold and silver jewelry" presented an innovative pendant by Helga Zahn. She had developed the surprising and unprecedented formal artistic language employed here (p. 28) from her stencil technique. Disk follows disk in this

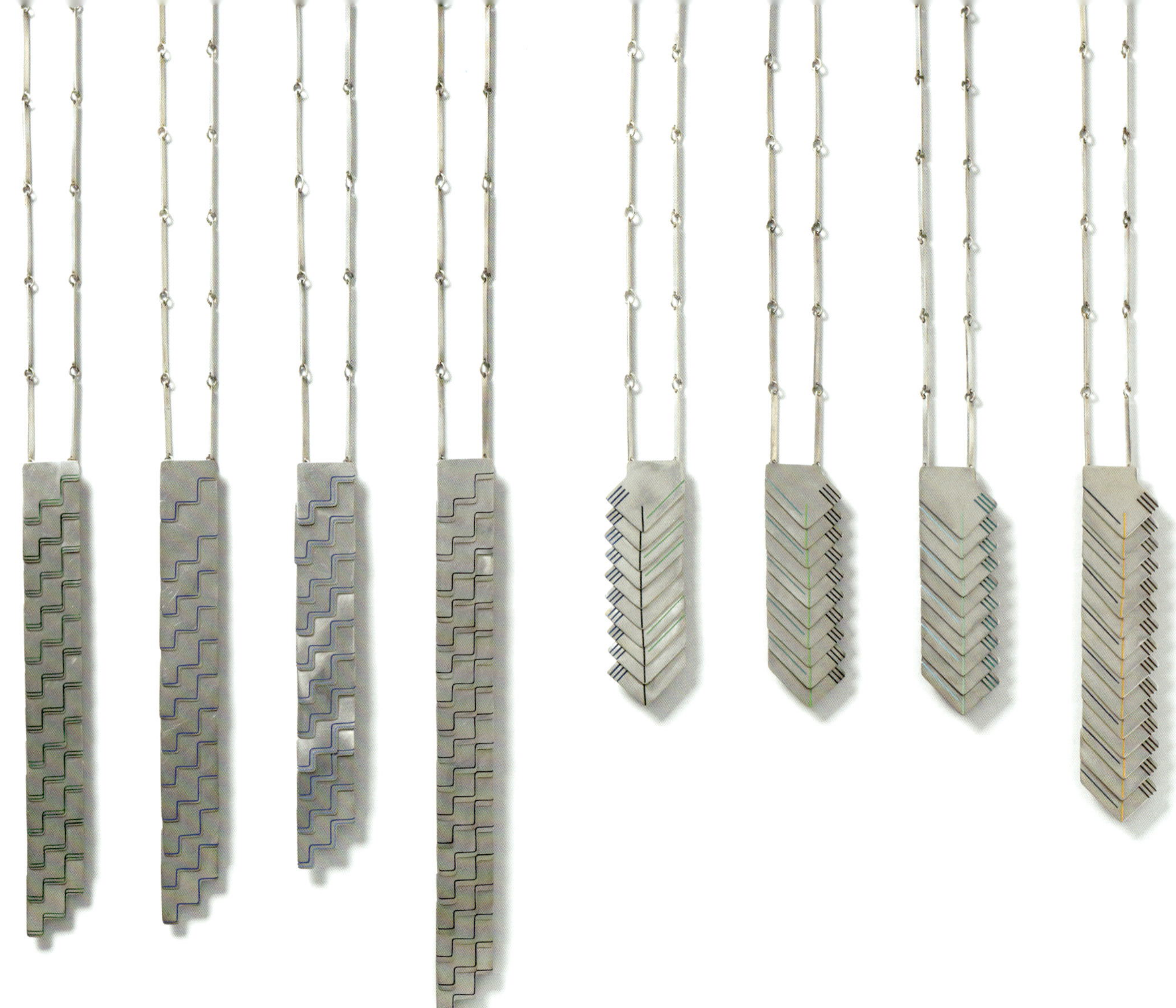

Anhänger | pendants, 1968–1971
Silber, Emaille | silver, enamel
H. 9–20,2 cm, B. 2–3 cm | h. 9–20,2 cm, w. 2–3 cm
Privatbesitz, Privatbesitz Monika Dölling, Privatsammlung, Die Neue Sammlung – The Design Museum. Dauerleihgabe der Danner-Stiftung München | Private property, private property Monika Dölling, private collection, Die Neue Sammlung – The Design Museum. Permanent loan of the Danner Foundation Munich

Guedes an einem 20-minütigen Experimentalfilm. Der Film „We Hope to Paint it Blue" wird 1970 auf der Eröffnungsvorstellung der 4. Hofer Filmtage im dortigen Central-Kino uraufgeführt. Und sie ist seit 1969 zu Gast auf den jährlich stattfindenden Ausstellungen „Schwarzenbacher Maler" und macht sich mit den „meist diskutierten Bildern"[16] einen Namen: „Spitzenklasse in ihren Siebdrucken (...) lässt Kreise und Exzenter in femininen Pop-Tönen streng formal aufgehen".[17] Die Aufenthalte in der Heimat lösen die Überlegung aus, Sommerkurse in Malerei, Grafik und Schmuck in Schwarzenbach anzubieten und damit gleichzeitig die dortigen Aufenthalte zu finanzieren.[18] Doch das Vorhaben scheitert.

1970 lädt Fritz Falk sie zu seiner Überblicksausstellung „Schmuck 70 – Tendenzen" ein. Als zweites Foto in der Kategorie „Individuell gestalteter Gold- und Silberschmuck", besticht ein neuartiger Anhänger Helga Zahns. Sie überrascht mit einer vollkommen neuen künstlerischen Sprache (S. 28), die sich aus ihrer Schablonentechnik heraus entwickelt hat. Plättchen reiht sich an Plättchen, übereinander montiert in unterschiedlicher Anzahl, in unterschiedlichen Formen und mit unterschiedlich zarten Emaille-Dekoren. Helga Zahn hat als logische Konsequenz aus ihrer Schablonentechnik einen System-Schmuck entwickelt, den es so in seiner Art noch nicht gegeben hat. Schnell findet der neuartige Schmuck offenbar auch das Interesse qualitativ hochwertiger Schmuckhersteller, wenngleich es am Ende doch nicht zu einer Zusammenarbeit kommt.[19] Das Außergewöhnliche und Neuartige des Schmucks wird in Kollegenkreisen schnell erkannt. Einladungen zu den wichtigen Großveranstaltungen der Zeit sind die Folge, wie z. B. zu „Sierraad 1900–1972" in Amersfoort oder auch 1971 die Einladung zur Eröffnungsausstellung der Electrum Gallery. Gegründet von Barbara Cartlidge und Ralph Turner genießt die heute nicht mehr existierende Galerie einen legendären Ruhm als weltweit erste Galerie, die sich ausschließlich dem Autorenschmuck widmete. Cartlidge gehörte bereits 1969 zu dem der Friedens- und Frauen-

piece, one mounted above the other in different numbers, shapes and varying, delicate enamel decors. As a logical consequence of her stencil technique, Helga Zahn developed a kind of system jewelry that was different from any kind previously made. And soon, high-end jewelry producers also began to take an interest in this novel kind of jewelry, even if ultimately no collaboration came about.[19] However, fellow jewelry artists recognized the unprecedented and exceptional nature of this jewelry straight away. This resulted in invitations to the key major events of the day, including "Sierraad 1900–1972" in Amersfoort, and her being asked to take part in the first exhibition held at the newly founded Electrum Gallery in 1971. Established by Barbara Cartlidge and Ralph Turner, the gallery, which no longer exists today, still enjoys a legendary reputation as the first gallery worldwide to exclusively show s tudio jewelry. As early as 1969, Cartlidge was a member of the founding collective of PACE Gallery in London, which was very open to the freedom and women's rights movements. In the same year Helga Zahn took part in the exhibition "Development of Modern Jewellery" held there. A small, exquisite catalog with great haptic qualities and a finely tuned color concept was made for the inaugural show at Electrum Gallery. Its layout was designed by London-based graphic designer Ray Carpenter and Helga Zahn. She was responsible in particular for the choice of paper and the three delicately coordinated colors.[20] The legendary logotype of Electrum Gallery could be admired on the cover of the catalog for the first time. Its design is somewhat similar to Helga Zahn's novel jewelry pendants (p. 100). As a gallery artist Helga Zahn also participated in the exhibitions staged in cooperation with Barbara Cartlidge: the show "British Jewellery" at Hanau's Goldschmiedehaus in 1973 and the presentation "Aspects of Jewellery" held at Aberdeen Art Gallery in Scotland.

Even before taking up her teaching post at the polytechnic Hornsey College of Art in Middlesex

bewegung sehr aufgeschlossenen Gründungskollektiv der Galerie PACE in London. Im selben Jahr beteiligt sich Helga Zahn dort an der Ausstellung „Development of Modern Jewellery". Für die Eröffnungsausstellung der Electrum Galerie entsteht ein kleiner, durch seine Haptik und die sensibel abgestimmte Farbigkeit bestechender Katalog. Verantwortlich für sein Layout: der in London lebende Grafiker Ray Carpenter und Helga Zahn. Ihr obliegt insbesondere die Wahl des Papiers und seiner drei, sehr fein aufeinander reagierenden Farben.[20] Zum ersten Mal ist der legendäre Schriftzug der Electrum Galerie auf dem Titel des Katalogs zu sehen. Er ist ähnlich gestaltet wie die neuartigen Schmuckanhänger von Helga Zahn (S. 100). Als Künstlerin der Galerie gehört Helga Zahn auch zum Teilnehmerkreis von Ausstellungen, die in Kooperation mit Barbara Cartlidge entstehen: 1973 die Ausstellung „British Jewellery" im Goldschmiedehaus Hanau und die Ausstellung „Aspects of Jewellery" in der Aberdeen Art Gallery in Schottland.

Noch vor ihrer 1974 beginnenden Lehrtätigkeit am Hornsey College of Art, Middlesex, Polytechnikum, lernt sie den technischen Assistenten des Schmuckbereichs kennen: „Ein Mann mit rund 40 Jahren mit einer Deutschen aus Weiden verheiratet, seit vielen Jahren arbeitet er in der Industrie (...). Ich machte ihm den Vorschlag mit mir im Team zu arbeiten und der Gedanke gefiel ihm".[21] Es handelt sich um Victor Ely, der ihr bei den Schmuckarbeiten in den kommenden Jahren zur Seite stehen wird. Seit den 60er-Jahren hat das Hornsey College grossen Einfluss darauf, wie und was an vielen britischen Kunsthochschulen im Bereich Schmuckdesign gelehrt wird. Verantwortlich für Thema und Inhalt am Hornsey College war Gerda Flöckinger. Sie legte in ihrem Unterricht den Schwerpunkt mehr auf Design und Forschung nach neuen Wegen als auf Verfahrenstechnik.[22] Man traut Helga Zahn am Hornsey Großes zu, wenn man sie bittet, die Nachfolgerin von Gerda Flöckinger zu werden, was sie selbst am meisten erstaunt, da sie, ohne Prüfungen abgelegt zu haben, nur aufgrund der Kenntnis ihrer Arbeiten eingestellt wird.[23] Nach einer, wie sie selbst

in the year 1974, she met the jewelry department's technical assistant: "A man of about 40 years of age, married to a German woman from Weiden, who has been working in the industry for many years (...). I proposed working together as a team and he likes the idea."[21] The man in question was Victor Ely, who was to lend his support to all of Zahn's jewelry work in the following years. From the 1960s onwards, Hornsey College was highly influential in terms of what was taught, and how, in the jewelry departments of many British art schools. Gerda Flöckinger was responsible for topics and material taught at Hornsey College. In her teaching, she placed a greater emphasis on design and research into new avenues than on methods.[22] And great things were expected of Helga Zahn when she was invited to succeed Gerda Flöckinger in Hornsey. Helga Zahn herself was utterly amazed to be employed in this position purely on the grounds of her work and as someone who had never passed any exams on the subject.[23] After what she herself described as being a small solo exhibition at Wales National Museum, she was included in the group show "The Craftsman's Art", organized jointly by the Crafts Advisory Committee and the Scottish Crafts Council in 1975/1976. The same year saw her being awarded funding from the Crafts Advisory Committee. This en-abled her to "broaden her technical knowledge in order to go in new directions".[24]

Ralph Turner, who abandoned the collaboration with Barbara Cartlidge in 1974, also struck out in new directions. As part of the Crafts Advisory Committee he now implemented his idea of a solo presentation of Helga Zahn's work. This had originally been planned as an exhibition at Electrum Gallery from May 17 through to June 24, 1972, but it had been cancelled. Helga Zahn's list of invitees read like a Who's Who of studio jewelry and included a "Mrs. Albert List from New York". The American art collector Vera List had previously bought a necklace by Helga Zahn in 1971.[25] In April 1976 Turner gave the opening

sagt, kleinen Einzelausstellung im Nationalmuseum Wales, folgt 1975/1976 die Teilnahme an der Ausstellung „The Craftsman's Art", gemeinsam veranstaltet vom Crafts Advisory Committee und dem Scottish Crafts Council. Im selben Jahr wird ihre Arbeit durch eine Förderung des Crafts Advisory Committee belohnt. Sie ermöglicht es ihr „to broaden her technical knowledge in order to go in new directions".[24]

Neue Wege ist auch Ralph Turner gegangen, der 1974 die Zusammenarbeit mit Barbara Cartlidge aufgibt. Er gehört dem Crafts Advisory Committee an und führt nun seine Idee einer Einzelausstellung über das Werk Helga Zahns durch. Sie war ursprünglich vom 17. Mai bis 24. Juni 1972 als Ausstellung der Galerie Electrum geplant, dann aber abgesagt worden. Helga Zahns Einladungsliste ist ein „Who is Who" des Autorenschmucks, darunter „Mrs. Albert List aus New York". Schon 1971 hatte die amerikanische Kunstsammlerin Vera List einen Halsschmuck von Helga Zahn erworben.[25] Im April 1976 eröffnet Turner die Ausstellung „Helga Zahn. A retrospective assessment 1960–1976. Jewellery, prints and drawings". Unter den namhaften Besuchern finden sich Alexander Dunbar, Direktor des Scottish Arts Council, J. Noel White vom Worlds Crafts Council sowie Sir Paul Reilly, Director of the Design Council, und David Coombs, Herausgeber des Magazins „Antique Collector". Begeistert fasst Coombs das Gesehene in einem Brief an Turner zusammen: „(...) and I must confess that I was really bowled over by its beauty and inventive use of materials (...). Although it is interesting that the pieces could obviously be appreciated for themselves as display items, which is very rarely the case in my opinion."[26]

Eine der wenigen Ausstellungsideen, die in diesem Jahr noch das Interesse von Helga Zahn weckt, ist die Loot-Ausstellung von 1976 in der Goldsmiths' Hall, London. Erdacht und durchgeführt wird die Ausstellung von Graham Hughes, der im Ausstellungskatalog schreibt: „An exhibition of new gold, silver, jewels, glass and medals for sale at under £50 with a section £50 – £100."[27] Eine Ausstellungsidee, mit der Hughes das Erfolgskonzept der in

speech for the exhibition "Helga Zahn. A retrospective assessment 1960 – 1976. Jewellery, prints and drawings". The prominent guests included Alexander Dunbar, director of the Scottish Arts Council, J. Noel White of the Worlds Crafts Council as well as Sir Paul Reilly, director of the Design Council and David Coombs, editor of "Antique Collector" magazine. Coombs enthusiastically summarized the event in a letter to Turner: "(...) and I must confess that I was really bowled over by its beauty and inventive use of materials (...). Although it is interesting that the pieces could obviously be appreciated for themselves as display items, which is very rarely the case in my opinion."[26]

One of the few other exhibition concepts to capture Helga Zahn's interest that year was the Loot exhibition of 1976 held at Goldsmiths' Hall, London. The exhibition was conceived and implemented by Graham Hughes, who wrote in the accompanying catalog: "An exhibition of new gold, silver, jewels, glass and medals for sale at under £50 with a section £50 – £100."[27] Hughes revived the highly successful concept of the exhibition series "The Wearable Movement: Modern jewelry under fifty dollars" staged in the US after World War II for his show concept. In the end, Helga Zahn was not among the 300 exhibitors. Her retrospective taking place at the same time seems finally to have been the deciding factor against her participation.

After this successful year in London, Helga Zahn left the British Isles for New York, returning to Europe for a short while only in 1978 to take part in a three-week summer course held by jewelry artist Bruno Martinazzi in Ansedonia, Italy.[28] In New York she enrolled at the Kulicke-Starck Academy of Jewelry Art in order to attend courses in traditional techniques (enameling, cloisonné, soldering). Two of the first pieces she enameled herself are now owned by Crafts Council in London and a private collector (p. 80). It seems to have been Austrian jewelry artist Fritz Maierhofer, whom Helga Zahn met in Cartlidge's circle of

Amerika nach dem Zweiten Weltkrieg entwickelten Ausstellungen „The Wearable Movement: Modern jewelry under fifty dollars" aufgreift. Am Ende wird Helga Zahn nicht zu den über 300 Ausstellern gehören. Ihre zeitgleich stattfindende Retrospektive scheint hier das ausschlaggebende Argument gegen eine Teilnahme gewesen zu sein.

Nach dem erfolgreichen Jahr in London verlässt Helga Zahn die britische Insel in Richtung New York. Nur kurz kehrt sie 1978 für einen dreiwöchigen Sommerkurs bei dem Schmuckkünstler Bruno Martinazzi in Ansedonia, Italien, nach Europa zurück.[28] In New York schreibt sie sich an der Kulicke-Starck Academy of Jewelry Art ein, an der sie Kurse in den traditionellen Techniken Emaillieren, Cloisonné, Löten belegt. Zwei ihrer ersten, selbst emaillierten Stücke befinden sich heute im Crafts Council in London und in Privatbesitz (S. 80). Wohl auf Vermittlung des österreichischen Schmuckkünstlers Fritz Maierhofer, den sie im Kreis der Cartlidge-Künstler kennengelernt hatte, wird Helga Zahn zu der von Peter Skubic kuratierten Ausstellung „International Jewellery 1900–1980" im Künstlerhaus Wien eingeladen.[29] Und auch hier macht ihr System-Schmuck, obwohl zu Beginn der 70er-Jahre entwickelt, immer noch Furore.

1980 ist das Jahr, in dem Helga Zahn schwer erkrankt. Fotos ihrer Schmuckarbeiten, die der damals führende britische Produktfotograf David Cripps vier Jahre zuvor im Auftrag von Ralph Turner für den Londoner Ausstellungskatalog angefertigt hatte, sind mit anderen seiner Aufnahmen 1980/1981 auf einer Wanderausstellung in England zu sehen. Das Crafts Advisory Committee zeigt Schmuckarbeiten von ihr auf Ausstellungen in Stoke-on-Trent 1981 und in der Ausstellung „Makers Eye" 1982 in London. Helga Zahn stirbt 1985. Damit endet das Leben einer außergewöhnlichen Schmuckkünstlerin zu früh, als dass sie noch zu Lebzeiten einen festen Platz unter den namhaften Schmuckkünstlern hätte einnehmen können. Ihr diesen Platz zuzuweisen, gilt es jetzt nachzuholen.

artists, who instigated her participation in the exhibition "International Jewellery 1900–1980" held at Vienna's Künstlerhaus and curated by Peter Skubic.[29] And her system jewelry, developed in the early 1970s, turned out to be a show-stopper there, too.

In 1980 Helga Zahn fell seriously ill. Photographs of her jewelry pieces, which David Cripps, the leading product photographer of the time, had been commissioned to make for the London exhibition catalog by Ralph Turner four years earlier, were shown as part of a traveling exhibition of his photos in the UK in 1980/1981. The Crafts Advisory Committee showed some of her jewelry pieces at an exhibition in Stoke-on-Trent in 1981 and at the "Makers Eye" show held in London in 1982. Helga Zahn died in 1985. The life of this extraordinary jewelry artist ended too early for her to firmly establish her place among the most noted jewelry artists of all time. It is high time to rectify this now by honoring her legacy.

*"Helga Zahn's work was very important to me.
I saw her strength and her vision in her pieces.
I saw the lovely order and formality of her designs.
Her making skills were not sophisticated nor did they need to be.
She worked with a high degree: painstaking and careful with the balance and structure of the pieces, often forming and linking large silver shapes."*

Wendy Ramshaw, Schmuckkünstlerin[30]

Weggefährten | Companions

ApoGee Studio, New York, USA (1970–1983)
Farbworkshop/Galerie. 504 La Guardia Place, New York. 1970 gegründet von Peter Gee. 1970 Ausst. Grafik und Malerei von Peter Gee. Siehe auch: Peter Gee. | Colour workshop/gallery. Founded in 1970 by Peter Gee. 1970 exh. art design and paintings by Peter Gee. See also: Peter Gee. (MS)

Axiom Gallery, London, Großbritannien
Galerie. 79 Duke Street, London. 1960er-Jahre Nigel Greenwood Galeriemanager. Ende 1960er / Beginn 1970er Antoinette Godkin Direktorin. | Gallery. 1960s Nigel Greenwood gallery manager. End of 1960s / beginning of 1970s Antoinette Godkin director. Ausst. | exh. Malcolm Morley (winner of the first Turner-Prize). 1966 Michael Tyzack and Reliif Constructions. 1967 works by Gillian Wise and 4 American Painters: George. Rankine. Reichek. Sterne. 1968 Richard Paul Lohse. 1943–1968 Helga Zahn, Kim Lim, Ian Hamilton Finlay, Michael Tyzack, John Plump et al. (MS)

Heinz Badewitz (26.05.1941 Hof, Deutschland – 10.03.2016 Graz, Österreich)
Filmschaffender, Festivalleiter. 1963 München, Studium am Deutschen Institut für Film und Fernsehen (heute Hochschule für Fernsehen und Film). Mitte 1960er-Jahre Kurzfilme. 1967 mit Uwe Brandner Initiierung und Leitung Hofer Filmtage. 1970 zur Eröffnung Hofer Filmtage Erstaufführung des Experimentalfilms „We Hope to Paint it Blue" von Eduardo Guedes und Helga Zahn. 1977–2010 kuratiert Reihe „German Cinema" auf der Berlinale. Filmmaker, festival director. 1963 Munich, studies at Deutsches Institut für Film und Fernsehen (today Hochschule für Fernsehen und Film). Mid-1960s short films. 1967 with Uwe Brandner founded and managed Hofer Filmtage. 1970 during opening of Hofer Filmtage first run of experimental film "We Hope to Paint it Blue" by Eduardo Guedes and Helga Zahn. 1977–2010 curator of "German Cinema" program at Berlinale. (PH)

Gijs Bakker (20.02.1942 Amersfoort, Niederlande – lebt und arbeitet in Amsterdam, Niederlande)
Schmuckkünstler, Industriedesigner. 1965 mit Emmy van Leersum Schmuckatelier „De Werfkelder", Utrecht. 1966–1986 tätig als Industriedesigner. Lehrtätigkeit: 1977–1978 Akademie voor Beeldende Kunsten, Arnhem. 1985–1987 Technische Hogeschool, Delft. 1987–2003 Academie voor Industriële Vormgeving, Eindhoven. Seit 2003 mit Renny Ramakers Leiter Master-Programm Interior, Industrial and Identity Design, Design Academy, Eindhoven.
Teilnahmen: 1968 Jablonec '68. II. Internationale Schmuckausstellung, Jablonec nad Nisou. 1970 Schmuck 70 – Tendenzen. Schmuckmuseum Pforzheim. 1972 Sieraad 1900–1972. Eerste Triennale. Zonnehof, Amersfoort. 1980 Schmuck International 1900–1980 Künstlerhaus Wien. 1991 The 20th Anniversary Show. Electrum Gallery, London. Auszeichnungen: 1966 Van de Rijn-Preis, 1968 mit Emmy van Leersum Gold- und Silbermedaille Internationale Schmuckausstellung, Jablonec nad Nidsou. 1984 Architekturpreis „De Fantasie". Almere, | Studio jewelry artist, industrial designer. 1965 with Emmy van Leersum jewelry atelier "De Werfkelder", Utrecht. 1966–1986 worked as industrial designer.
Teaching: 1971–1978 Akademie voor Beeldende Kunsten, Arnhem. 1985–1987 Technische Hogeschool. Delft. 1987–2003 Academie voor Industriële Vormgeving, Eindhoven. Since 2003 with Renny Ramakers head of the master program Interior, Industrial and Identity Design, Design Academy, Eindhoven. Participations: 1968 Jablonec '68. II. International Jewellery Exhibition, Jablonec nad Nisou. 1970 Schmuck 70 – Tendenzen. Schmuckmuseum Pforzheim. 1972 Sieraad 1900–1972. Eerste Triennale. Zonnehof, Armersfoort. 1980 Schmuck International 1900–1980 Künstlerhaus Vienna. The 20th Anniversary show. Electrum Gallery, London. Awards: 1966 Van de Rijn-Award. 1968 with Emmy van Leersum Gold- and Silver Medal International Jewellery Exhibition, Jablonec nad Nisou. 1984 architecture award "De Fantasie", Almere. (EL)

Gene Baro, geb. als Eugene Barott, seit 1950 Gene Baro (12.01.1924 New York, NY, USA – 15.11.1982 Old Bennington, VT, USA)
Kurator, Lektor, Kunstkritiker. 1963 England. Korrespondent für Art in America, Art International und Studio International. Hg. Art International Magazin, Lugano. 1969/1970 New York. Bis 1972 Direktor und 1974–1976 Berater Corcoran Gallery, Washington. Berater Government Research Corporation. Hg. National Journal. Lehrtätigkeit: Universität Florida. 1960er-Jahre Vorlesungen an europäischen Universitäten. Ausst. für Corcoran Gallery und Brooklyn Museum: Paul Jenkins, Anni Albers, David Hockney, Sol LeWitt und 1976 America on Stage: 200 Years of Performing Art. Kennedy Centre, Washington.

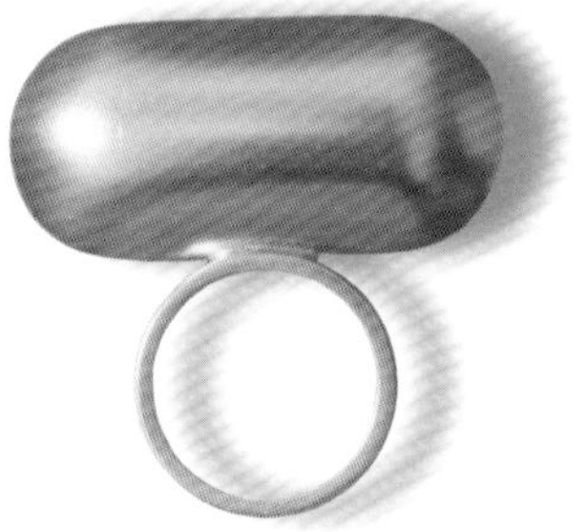
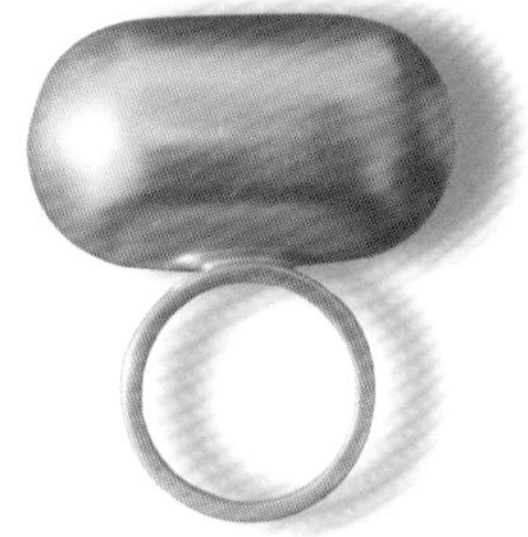
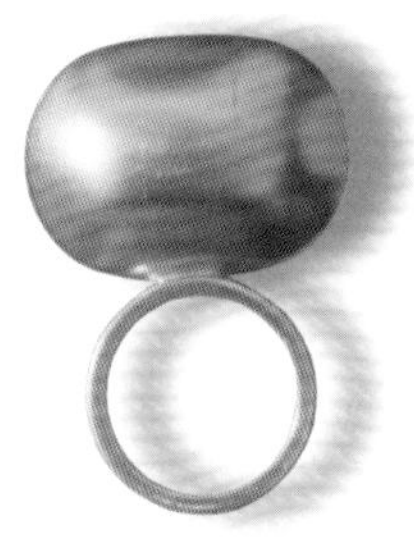

Ringset | ring set, 1969
Silber | silver
Foto: Archiv Helga Zahn

1976/1977 Thirty Years of American Printmaking. Brooklyn Museum, New York. 1980/1981 American Drawings in Black and White: 1970–1980. Brooklyn Museum/Carnegie International, Pittsburgh. | Curator, lecturer, art critic. 1963 Great Britain. Correspondent for Art in America. Art International and Studio International magazines. Senior editor of Art International magazine, Lugano. 1969/1970 New York. Until 1972 director and 1974–1976 consultant Corcoran Gallery, Washington. Consultant to the Government Research Corporation. Associate editor of the National Journal. Teaching: University of Florida. During 1960s lectured at European universities. Exh. at Corcoran Gallery and Brooklyn Museum: Paul Jenkins, Anni Albers, David Hockney, Sol LeWitt and 1976 America on Stage: 200 Years of Performing Art. Kennedy Centre, Washington. 1976/1977 Thirty Years of American Printmaking. Brooklyn Museum, New York. 1980/1981 American Drawings in Black and White: 1970–1980. Brooklyn Museum/Carnegie International, Pittsburgh. (MS)

Friedrich Becker (25.05.1922 Ende bei Herdecke, Deutschland – 15.05.1997 Düsseldorf, Deutschland) Goldschmied. Lehrtätigkeit: 1952–1981 Werkkunstschule/Fachhochschule Düsseldorf. Auszeichnungen: 1959 Bayerischer Staatspreis Internationale Handwerksmesse München. 1973 Verdienstorden der Bundesrepublik Deutschland. 1987 Deutscher Schmuck- und Edelsteinpreis, Idar-Oberstein. 1990 Ehrenmitglied „Forum für Schmuck und Design", Köln. 1997 angedacht für Ehrendoktor-Würde vom Royal College of Art, London. | Goldsmith. Teaching: 1952–1981 Werkkunstschule/Fachhochschule Dusseldorf. Awards: 1959 Bayerischer Staatspreis Internationale Handwerksmesse München. 1973 The Order of Merit of the Federal Republic of Germany. 1987 Deutscher Schmuck- und Edelsteinpreis, Idar-Oberstein. 1990 Honorary Member "Forum für Schmuck und Design", Cologne. 1997 chosen to receive an Honarary Doctorate of the Royal College of Art, London.

Ernst Berk (12.10.1909 Köln, Deutschland – 30.09.1993 Berlin, Deutschland)
Solotänzer, Choreograf, Komponist, Schauspieler. Ausbildung am Wigman-Institut, Köln. Ballett für Max Reinhardt zu den Salzburger Festspielen. 1934 London. 1935 Ballette für Covent Garden und West End Produktionen. 1946 mit Nesta Brooking Gründung Dance Theater. 1955 Studio für elektronische Musik. Lehrtätigkeit: seit 1985 Hochschule der Künste, Berlin. Auszeichnung: 1947 Ehrendiplom für Ballett „Tilustrum". Choreographic Competition, Kopenhagen. | Solo dancer, choreographer, composer, actor. Education at Wigman Institute, Cologne. Ballet for Max Reinhardt during Salzburg Festival. 1934 London. 1935 ballets for Covent Garden and West End productions. 1946 together with Nesta Brooking founder of Dance Theater. 1955 studio for electronic music. Teaching: since 1985 Hochschule der Künste, Berlin. Award: 1947 honorable diploma for the ballet "Tilustrum". Choreographic Competition, Copenhagen. (MS)

Irena Brynner (1917 Wladiwostok, Russland – 2002 New York, NY, USA) Goldschmiedin. Schmuckkünstlerin. 1946 San Francisco, CA. 1957 New York. 1972–1984 Schweiz/USA. 1957 Studio New York, Lehrtätigkeit: 1962–1969 (?) Department of Adult Education am Museum of Modern Art, New York. 1984 Craft Students League YWCA, New York. Teilnahmen: 1959 Museum of Contemporary Crafts of New York. 1979 Renwick Gallery, Washington D.C. Auszeichnung: 1963 Bayerischer Staatspreis Internationale Handwerksmesse München. | Goldsmith, studio jewelry artist. 1946 San Francisco, CA. 1957 New York, 1972–1984 Switzerland/USA. 1957 studio New York. Teaching: 1962–1969 (?) Department of Education at Museum of Modern Art, New York.

1984 Craft Students League at the YWCA, New York. Participations: 1959 Museum of Contemporary Crafts of New York. 1979 Renwick Gallery, Washington D.C. Award: 1963 Bayerischer Staatspreis Internationale Handwerksmesse München.

Vivianna Torun Bülow-Hübe (04.12.1927 Malmö, Schweden – 03.07.2004 Kopenhagen, Dänemark)
Schmuckkünstlerin, -designerin. 1948–1956 Atelier in Schweden. 1956–1968 Atelier in Paris und Biot. Kontakt mit Pablo Picasso. Schmuckentwürfe für Brigitte Bardot. Ingrid Bergman. Billie Holiday. Seit 1967 Arbeit mit Georg Jensen, Kopenhagen. 1968–1978 Atelier in Wolfsburg. 1978–2003 Jakarta. Teilnahmen: 1951, 1954, 1960 Triennale di Milano. 1961 Goldsmiths' Hall. Victoria & Albert Museum, London. 1962 Weltausstellung Seattle. 1967 Weltausstellung Montréal. Auszeichnungen: 1954 Silbermedaille X. Triennale di Milano. 1960 Goldmedaille XII. Triennale di Milano und Frederik-Lunning-Preis für Design, New York. 1992 Prinz-Eugen-Medaille, Schweden | Jewelry artist, jewelry designer. 1948–1956 studio in Sweden. 1956–1968 studio in Paris and Biot. Contact with Pablo Picasso. Jewelry designs for Brigitte Bardot, Ingrid Bergman and Billie Holiday. Since 1967 working with Georg Jensen, Copenhagen. 1968–1978 studio in Wolfsburg. 1978–2003 Jakarta. Participations: 1951, 1954, 1960 Triennale di Milano. 1961 Goldsmiths' Hall. Victoria & Albert Museum, London. 1962 Expo Seattle. 1967 Expo Montréal. Awards: 1954 Silver Medal X. Triennale di Milano. 1960 Gold Medal XII. Triennale di Milano and Frederik Lunning Award for Design, New York. 1992 Prinz Eugen Medal, Sweden. (PH)

James Burr (geb. 1926)
Maler, Grafiker. 1960er-Jahre Studium Goldsmith College, London. Leiter des Art Department. City Literary Institute, London. | Painter, graphic artist. 1960s studies at Goldsmith College, London. Head of Art Department. City Literary Institute, London. (PH)

Ray Carpenter (1942 London, Großbritannien – lebt und arbeitet in London, Großbritannien)
Fotograf, Grafiker, Maler. 1964 Unterzeichner Manifest „First Things First". 1971–2012 Grafiker für Arts Council, Crafts Advisory Committee, Crafts Council, British Council, Henry Moore Institute, Electrum Gallery, Mikron Theatre Company. 1971 mit Helga Zahn Eröffnungskatalog Gallery Electrum, London. 1976 Katalog Helga Zahn. A Retrospective Assessment 1960 – 1976. Jewellery. Prints and Drawings. London. Lehrtätigkeit: 1970–1972 College of Art, Canterbury. 1971–1981 Chelsea College of Arts, London. | Photographer, graphic designer, painter. 1964 signs the manifest "First Things First". 1971–2012 graphic designer. Clients included Arts Council, Crafts Advisory committee, Crafts Council, British Council, Henry Moore Institute, Electrum Gallery, Mikron Theatre Company. 1971 with Helga Zahn catalog for the opening exh. of Electrum Gallery , London. 1976 catalog Helga Zahn. A Retrospective Assessment 1960–1976. Jewellery. Prints and Drawings. London. Teaching: 1970–1972 College of Art, Canterbury. 1971–1981 Chelsea College of Arts, London. (MS)

Barbara Cartlidge (1922 Berlin, Deutschland – lebt in London, Großbritannien)
Goldschmiedin, Galeristin. 1938 London. 1969 Mitbegründerin PACE Gallery. Kennenlernen von Ralph Turner. 1971 mit Turner Eröffnung Electrum Gallery, 1971–2007 Leitung der Galerie, 2007 Verkauf der Galerie. Teilnahmen: 1960 Heals, London. 1969 Development of Modern Jewellery. PACE Gallery, London. 1971 British Design. Louvre, Paris. 1972 Internationale Handwerksmesse München. | Goldsmith, Gallery owner. 1938 London. 1969 co-founder of PACE Gallery. Contact with Ralph Turner. 1971 with Turner establishing Electrum Gallery, 1971–2007 gallery director, 2007 sells gallery. Participations: 1960 Heals, London. 1969 Development of Modern Jewellery. PACE Gallery, London. 1971 British Design. Louvre, Paris. 1972 Internationale Handwerksmesse München. (MS)

Anton Cepka (17.01.1936 Šulekovo, ČSSR – lebt und arbeitet in Svätý Jur/Bratislava, Slowakische Republik) Schmuckkünstler. 1967–1970 Mitglied im „Klub konkretistů", Prag. Lehrtätigkeit: 1990 Einrichtung Klasse für Metall und Schmuck, Hochschule für Bildende Kunst und Design (VŠVU), Bratislava. 1993 Kunstdozent an VŠVU. 2001 Ehrendoktorwürde der VŠVU. Teilnahmen: 1964 Internationale Handwerksmesse München. 1968 I. Internationales Symposium für Silberschmuck, Jablonec nad Nisou. 1970 Schmuck 70 – Tendenzen. Schmuckmuseum Pforzheim. 1971 Gold + Silber. Schmuck + Gerät von Albrecht Dürer bis zur Gegenwart. Norishalle, Nürnberg. 1980 Schmuck International 1900–1980. Künstlerhaus Wien. Auszeichnungen: 1964 Bayerischer Staatspreis Internationale Handwerksmesse München. 1967 Cyprián-Majerník-Preis. 1977 Gold- und 1980 Silbermedaille Internationale Bijouterieausstellung, Jablonec nad Nisou. 1990 Goldener Ehrenring der Gesellschaft für Goldschmiedekunst, Hanau.

Studio jewelry artist.
1967–1970 member of "Klub konkretistů", Prague. Teaching: 1990 established the class for metal and jewelry, Academy of Fine Arts and Design (VŠVU), Bratislava. 1993 art-lecturer at VŠVU, 2001 honorary doctorate by VŠVU. Participations: 1964 Internationale Handwerksmesse München. 1968 I. International Symposium for Silver Jewelry, Jablonec nad Nisou. 1970 Schmuck 70 – Tendenzen. Schmuckmuseum Pforzheim. 1971 Gold + Silber. Schmuck + Gerät von Albrecht Dürer bis zur Gegenwart. Norishalle, Nuremberg. 1980 Schmuck International 1900–1980. Künstlerhaus Vienna, Austria. Awards: 1964 Bayerischer Staatspreis Internationale Handwerksmesse München. 1967 Cyprián Majerník Award, Bratislava. 1977 gold medal and 1980 silver medal International Bijouterie Exhibition, Jablonec nad Nisou. 1990 Goldener Ehrenring Gesellschaft für Goldschmiedekunst, Hanau. (EL)

David Coombs (1937 Großbritannien)
Autor, Kunsthistoriker, Lehrer. 1974–1994 Herausgeber Antique Collector. Kolumnist für Antiques Trade Gazette. 1999 Onlinepublikation ArtNewsLetter.com. I Author, art historian, teacher. 1974–1994 editor Antique Collector magazine. Columnist for Antiques Trade Gazette. 1999 publication ArtNewsLetter.com. (MS)

David Cripps (30.04.1938 London, Großbritannien – 20.01.2013 Ramsgate, Großbritannien)
(Produkt-) Fotograf. 1973 Crafts Magazin. 1975 Sunday Times. Tätig u.a. für Crafts Council, Design Magazine. (Product-) Photographer. 1973 Crafts magazine. 1975 Sunday Times magazine. Working i. a. for Crafts Council and design magazines. (MS)

Hans Werner Cullmann (Mörschried)
Handel mit Edelsteinen und Gemmen. I Trade with stones gems. (PH)

Alexander Dunbar (12.03.1930 London, Großbritannien – 2012)
Anwalt. 1963 Gründung North Eastern Association for the Arts, Newcastle. 1970–1971 UK-Direktor Gulbenkian Foundation. 1971–1980 Direktor Scottish Arts Council. Lawyer. 1963 founded North Eastern Association for the Arts, Newcastle. 1970–1971 UK director Gulbenkian Foundation. 1971–1980 director Scottish Arts Council. (MS)

Victor Ely
(geb. Anfang 1930er-Jahre)
1970er-Jahre technischer Assistent Schmuckdepartment Hornsey College of Art, Middlesex. 1973 Assistent von Helga Zahn. I 1970s technical assistant Jewelry Department Hornsey College of Art, Middlesex. 1973 assistant to Helga Zahn. (PH)

Max Fröhlich (16.12.1908 Ennenda, Kanton Glarus, Schweiz – 1997 Zürich, Schweiz)
Gold-, Silberschmied. 1928–1932 Werkstatt Arnold Stockmal, Luzern. 1929–1930 Wolfers Frères, Brüssel. 1932 Heinrich Eggs, Zürich. 1933 Assistent von Martin Johann Vermeulen. Metallklasse Kunstgewerbeschule Zürich. 1934–1945 Werkstatt Zürich (seit 1937 mit Otto Kraska). Lehrtätigkeit: 1945–1966 Leiter Metallklasse und 1948–1972 Rektor Kunstgewerbeschule Zürich. 1955 „Lehrbuch für Goldschmiede". 1963–1970 Gastdozent an Hochschulen in Belgien und Ghana. 1963–1969 Delegierter des ICSID-Kongresses und 1966–1980 des World Crafts Council. Teilnahmen: 1966 Internationale Handwerksmesse München. 1968 Jablonec '68. II. Internationale Schmuckausstellung, Jablonec nad Nisou. 1970 Schmuck 70 – Tendenzen, Schmuckmuseum Pforzheim. 1971 Gold + Silber. Schmuck + Gerät von Albrecht Dürer bis zur Gegenwart. Norishalle, Nürnberg. 1980 Schmuck International 1900–1980, Künstlerhaus Wien. Auszeichnungen: 1965 Goldener Ehrenring der Gesellschaft für Goldschmiedekunst, Hamburg. 1966 Bayerischer Staatspreis Internationale Handwerksmesse München und Berufung zum Bachelor of Art der University of Sience and Technology, Kumasi. I Gold-, silversmith. 1928–1932 studio Arnold Stockmal, Lucerne. 1929–1930 Wolfers Frères, Brussels. 1932 Heinirch Eggs, Zurich. 1933 assisted Martin Johann Vermeulen, metal class. Kunstgewerbeschule Zurich. 1934–1945 studio in Zurich (since 1937 with Otto Kraska). Teaching: 1945–1966 head of metal class and 1948–1972 rector of Kunstgewerbeschule Zurich. 1955 "Lehrbuch für Golschmiede". 1963–1970 guest lecturer at universities in Belgium and Ghana. 1963–1969 deputy of ICSID-Congress and 1966–1980 of World Crafts Council. Participations: 1966 Internationale Handwerksmesse München. 1968 Jablonec '68. II. International Jewellery Exhibition, Jablonec nad Nisou. 1970 Schmuck 70 – Tendenzen, Schmuckmuseum Pforzheim. 1971 Gold + Silber. Schmuck + Gerät von Albrecht Dürer bis zur Gegenwart. Norishalle, Nuremberg. 1980 Schmuck International 1900–1980 Künstlerhaus Vienna. Awards: 1965 Goldener Ehrenring, Gesellschaft für Goldschmiedekunst, Hamburg. 1966 Bayerischer Staatspreis Internationale Handwerksmesse München and appointed to Bachelor of Art of the University of Sience and Technology, Kumasi. (EL)

Anton Frühauf (08.06.1914 Meran, Italien – 02.01.1999 Meran, Italien)

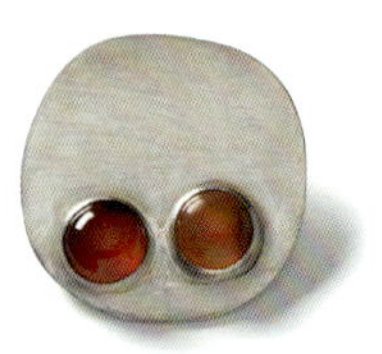
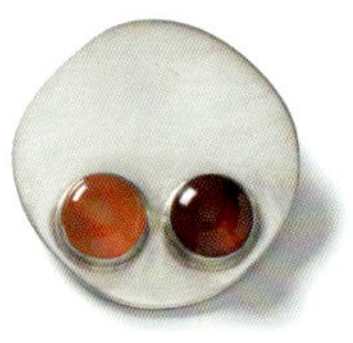

Manschettenknöpfe | cufflinks, 1961
Silber, Achate | silver, agates
H. 2,9 cm, B. 2,8 cm | h. 2,9 cm, w. 2,8 cm
Privatbesitz | private property

Juwelier, Grafiker, Karikaturist. 1935–1936 Juweliergeschäft „Corso Umberto" von Davide Ventrella, Rom. 1937–1941 Juweliergeschäft Weisshaupt, München. 1961 Übernahme des väterlichen Juweliergeschäfts, Meran. Teilnahmen: 1957, 1963 und 1984 Internationale Handwerksmesse München. Auszeichnungen: 1957 Bayerischer Staatspreis Internationale Handwerksmesse München. 1968 Österreichischer Staatspreis. 1980 Goldmedaille, Ordre de St. Fortunat, Mainz. 1984 Bayerischer Staatspreis Internationale Handwerksmesse München. | Jeweler, graphic artist, caricaturist. 1935–1936 jeweler shop "Corso Umberto" of Davide Ventrella, Rome. 1937–1941 jewelershop Weisshaupt, Munich. 1961 takes over his father's jeweler shop, Meran. Participations: 1957, 1963 and 1984 Internationale Handwerksmesse München. Awards: 1957 Bayerischer Staatspreis Internationale Handwerksmesse München. 1968 Österreichischer Staatspreis. 1980 Gold Medal, Ordre de St. Fortunat, Mainz. 1984 Bayerischer Staatspreis Internationale Handwerksmesse München. (EL)

Electrum Gallery (1971–2007 Moulton Street, London. Großbritannien)
1971 Gründung durch Barbara Cartlidge und Ralph Turner. Katalog und Gestaltung Eröffnungsausstellung Helga Zahn und Ray Carpenter. Ausst. u. a.: Giampaolo Babetto, Claus Bury, Anton Cepka, Gerda Flöckinger, Yasuki Hiramatsu, Helfried Kodré. Fritz Maierhofer, E. R. Nele, Wendy Ramshaw, David Watkins. | 1971 founded by Barbara Cartlidge and Ralph Turner. Catalog and design opening exhibition Helga Zahn and Ray Carpenter. Exh. et al.: Giampaolo Babetto, Claus Bury, Anton Cepka, Gerda Flöckinger, Yasuki Hiramatsu, Helfried Kodré, Fritz Maierhofer, E. R. Nele. Wendy Ramshaw, David Watkins. (PH)

Galerie Richard Foncke (1967–1997 Spijkstraat, Gent, Belgien)
Ausst. u. a. | exh. et al.: 1968 Pol Mara. Royer Raveel, Luc Peire. 1970 Helga Zahn. 1971 Graphique = Plexi + Formicacreations. 1972 Dieter Roth. 1979 Emmy van Leersum. (DA)

Peter Gee (1932 Leicestershire, Großbritannien – 2005 Boston, MA, USA)
Pop-Art-Künstler, Designer. 1962 USA. 1970 Gründung ApoGee Studio, New York, NY. Lehrtätigkeit: 1958 Basic Design, London. School of Visual Arts und New School, New York. Harvard School of Architecture, Cambridge. Teilnahmen: 1968 World and Image. Museum of Modern Art, New York. 1970 ApoGee Studio, New York. 1970 Galerie Weinelt, Hof. | Pop artist, designer. 1962 USA. 1970 founded ApoGee Studio, New York. Teaching: 1958 Basic Design, London. School of Visual Arts and New School, New York. Harvard School of Architecture, Cambridge. Participations: 1968 World and Image. Museum of Modern Art, New York. 1970 ApoGee Studio, New York. 1970 Galerie Weinelt, Hof. (MS)

Felix Giacomoni (1965–1971)
Verwaltungsmitarbeiter. 1968 stellvertretender Leiter und 1969–1971 Leiter des Théâtre des Nations, später Théâtre National de l'Odéon, Paris. 1969–1970 und 1975–1976 verantwortlich für Werbung (Plakate). 1978–1986 stellvertretender Leiter des französischen Nationalarchivs, Paris. | 1965–1971 administrator. 1968 deputy director and 1969–1971 director of Théâtre des Nations, Théâtre National de l'Odéon, Paris. 1969–1970 and 1975–1976 responsible for advertising (posters). 1978–1986 deputy director of National Archives of France, Paris. (DA)

Nicholas Grimshaw
(09.10.1939 Hove, Großbritannien – lebt und arbeitet in London, Großbritannien)
Architekt. 1959–1962 Edinburgh. 1962–1965 London. 1962/1963 Kennenlernen von Helga Zahn. 1965 Büro mit Terry Farrell, London. 1980 „Nicholas Grimshaw & Partners", London. Lehrtätigkeit: 1972–1973 Bartlett School, University of London. 1978–1979 Cambridge University. | Architect. 1959–1962 Edinburgh. 1962–1965 London. 1962/1963 gets to know Helga Zahn. 1965 company with Terry Farrell, London. 1980 "Nicholas Grimshaw & Partners", London. Teaching: 1972–1973

Bartlett School, University of London. 1978–1979 Cambridge University. (DA)

Tessa Grimshaw-Traeger (1938 Guildford Surrey, Großbritannien – lebt und arbeitet in London, Großbritannien)
Produkt-Fotografin. 1954–1958 Guildford. 1959 London. 1959/1960 Kennenlernen von Helga Zahn. 1960 New York, NY. 1959–1962 Arbeit für Queen Magazine, Observer, Tatler, London. 1962–1964 Studio: Marshall Street 1, London. 1964–1965 arbeitet mit Modefotograf Ronald Traeger, Paris. 1965–1988 Atelier Rossetti Studios, London. 1967 (?) Arbeit für Vogue, London. 1971 Mitglied Association of Fashion. Advertising and Editorial Photographers. 1975–1991 Arbeit mit Arabella Boxer für Vogue, London. I Product photographer. 1954–1958 Guildford. 1959 London. 1959/1960 contact with Helga Zahn. 1960 New York, NY. 1964–1965 working together with fashion photographer Ronald Traeger, Paris. 1959–1962 working for Queen Magazine, Observer, Tatler London. 1962–1964 studio at Marshall Street 1, London. 1964–1965 working together with fashion photographer Ronald Traeger, Paris. 1965–1988 studio Rossetti Studios, London. 1967 (?) worked for Vogue, London. 1971 member Association of Fashion. Advertising and Editorial Photographers. 1975–1991 worked with Arabella Boxer for Vogue, London. (DA)

Eduardo Luis Santos Correia Guedes (21.04.1941 Lissabon, Portugal – 29.08.2000 Lissabon, Portugal) Filmregisseur, Filmproduzent. 1961 London. 1963 Kennenlernen von Helga Zahn. 1964 International Film School, London. 1965 Dokumentarfilme in Brasilien. 1968 Cutter- und Regisseurtätigkeit. 1971 Mitglied „Cinema Action", London. 1974 Portugal. 1974–1976 Mitglied Independent Film-Makers Association, London. 1982 Mitbegründer Channel 4, London. Filme: 1963 Duet. 1969 Not a Penny on the Rent. 1970 We Hope to Paint it Blue (mit Helga Zahn). Praise Marx und Pass the Ammunition. 1981 So That You Can Live. 1986 Rocinante. 1989 Bearskin. Auszeichnungen: 1994 Nominierung Goldener Leopard, Locarno International Film Festival. I Film director, film producer. 1961 London. 1963 contact with Helga Zahn. 1964 International Film School London. 1965 documentaries in Brasil. 1968 cutter und film director. 1971 member "Cinema Action", London. 1974 Portugal. 1974–1976 Fellow of Independent Film-Makers Association, London. 1982 co-founder of Channel 4, London. Films: 1963 Duet. 1969 Not a Penny on the Rent. 1970 We Hope to Paint it Blue (with Helga Zahn). Praise Marx and Pass the Ammunition. 1981 So That You can Live. 1986 Rocinante. 1989 Bearskin. Awards: 1994 nominated for Golden Leopard, Locarno International Film Festival. (PH)

Herbert Hofmann (1899 Leipzig, Deutschland – 1971 München, Deutschland) Volkswirt. Kunsthistoriker. Seit 1930 Publikationen über Innenarchitektur. 1943 München. 1950 Deutscher Werkbund (DWB). 1952/1953 Geschäftsführer DWB. 1952 Handwerkspfleger von Bayern. 1955 Film „Werk der Hände". 1958 deutsche Auswahl Kunsthandwerk, Weltausstellung Brüssel. 1959 initiiert Schmuck-Ausstellungen Internationale Handwerksmesse München. I Economist. Art historian. Since 1930 publications on interior design. 1943 Munich. 1950 Deutscher Werkbund (DWB). 1952/1953 Managing Director of DWB. 1952 Bavarian crafts curator. 1955 film "Werk der Hände". 1958 responsible for the German crafts collection, Expo Brussels. 1959 initiated jewelry exhibitions Internationale Handwerksmesse München. (PH)

Tom Hudson (03.07.1922 Hordon, Großbritannien – 27.12.1997 Bristol, Großbritannien)

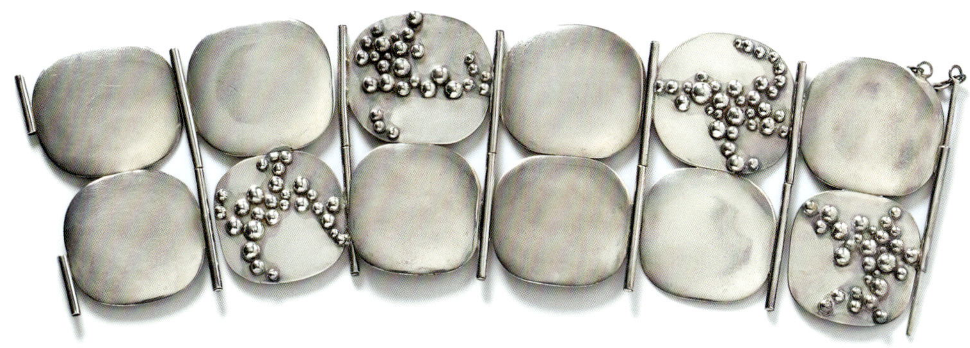

Armschmuck I bracelet, 1965
Silber I silver
H. 6,9 cm, L. 24 cm
h. 6,9 cm, l. 24 cm
Privatsammlung München
private collection Munich

Künstler. Mitte 1940er-Jahre Paris. Lehrtätigkeit: King's College, Newcastle (heute University of Newcastle upon Tyne). Courtauld Institute, London. 1951 Malerei an Lowestoft School of Art, Suffolk (heute Lowestoft College). 1954 und 1956 Sommerkurse in Scarborough mit Harry Thubron, Victore Pasmore. 1956 Lehrer bei Harry Thubron, Leeds College of Art. 1960 Leiter Foundation Studies am Leicester College of Art. 1964–1977 Director of Studies Cardiff College of Art, später Dekan am Emily Carr College of Art and Design, Vancouver. Teilnahmen: 1963 The Visual Adventure. Drian Galleries, London und 1964 Education Department. Museum of Modern Art, New York. Artist. Mid 1940s Paris. Teaching: King's College, Newcastle (today University of Newcastle upon Tyne). Courtauld Institute, London. 1951 Painting at Lowestoft School of Art, Suffolk (today Lowestoft College). 1954 and 1956 summer school in Scarborough with Harry Thubron, Victore Pasmore. 1956 teaching with Harry Thubron at Leeds College of Art. 1960 Head of Foundation Studies, Leicester College of Art. 1964–1977 Director of Studies at Cardiff College of Art, later dean of Emily Carr College of Art and Design, Vancouver. Participations: 1963 The Visual Adventure. Drian Galleries, London and 1964 Education Department. Museum of Modern Art, New York. (PH)

George Graham McKenny Hughes (17.04.1926 USA – 05.10.2010 Großbritannien)
Kunstadministrator, Ausstellungsmacher, Autor. 1951 Sekretär, später Art Director der Worshipful Company of Goldsmiths, London. 1961 erwirbt Studentenausstellung der Hornsey School of Art (Organisation Gerda Flöckinger), die Grundlage ist für Schmucksammlung der Worshipful Company und für Publikation „Modern Jewellery: An International Survey". 1965 Vorsitz Crafts Center Great Britain. 1973–1981 beratender Direktor für Kunst, Royal Mint. 1981–1991 Eigentümer Arts Review, gründet Crafts Center in Tokio, Nordamerika und Australien. Ausst.: 1961 International Exhibition of Modern Jewellery 1890–1961. Victoria & Albert Museum, London. 1968 Gerda Flöckinger. 1969 Ann Sutton. 1973 Medals Today. Goldsmiths Hall, London. Arts administrator, exhibition curator, author. 1951 secretary, later Art Director of Worshipful Company of Goldsmiths, London. 1961 bought exhibition of students' work, organized by Gerda Flöckinger (Hornsey School of Art) which became the base for the Worshipful Company's collection of studio jewelry and the book "Modern Jewellery: An International Survey". 1965 chairman Crafts Center Great Britain. 1973–1981 Consultant art director, Royal Mint. 1981–1991 owner of Arts Review, established Crafts Centers in Tokyo, North-America and Australia. Exh.: 1961 International Exhibition of Modern Jewellery 1890–1961. Victoria & Albert Museum, London. 1968 Gerda Flöckinger. 1969 Ann Sutton. 1973 Medals Today. Goldsmiths Hall, London. (PH)

Robert M. Kulicke (1924 Philadelphia, PA, USA – 14.12.2007 Manhattan, NY, USA)
Maler, Goldschmied, Entwerfer. Ende 1940er-Jahre Paris (G.I.Bill-Programm). Studium bei Fernand Léger. 1951 Geschäft „Kulicke Frames", New York. 1956 Aluminium-Rahmen für Museum of Modern Art (MOMA), New York. Ende 1950er-Jahre „schwebender" Rahmen für Knoll International. 1960 Acrylrahmen für Fotografie Department, MOMA. 1968 perfektioniert Granulationstechnik. 1970 verlässt „Kulicke Frames". Unterrichtet Granulationstechnik an Scarsdale Studio Workshop School, später im Kulicke Cloisonné Workshop. 1974 mit Jean Stark Gründung Kulicke-Stark Academy for Jewelry (1984 Umbenennung in Jewelry Arts Institute). 1982 assoziiertes und 1994 ordentliches Mitglied National Academy of Design, New York (heute National Academy Museum and School). I Painter, goldsmith, designer. End of 1940s Paris (G.I.Bill-program). Studies with Fernand Léger. 1951 shop "Kulicke Frames", New York. 1956 Aluminum Frame for Museum of Modern Art (MOMA), end of 1950s Floating Frame for Knoll International. 1960 Lucite Frame for MOMA's photography department. 1968 perfection of the granulation technique. 1970 leaves "Kulicke Frame". Teaches granulation technique at Scarsdale Studio Workshop School, later at Kulicke Cloisonné Workshop. 1974 with Jean Stark founding of the Kulicke-Academy for Jewelry (since 1984 Jewelry Arts Institute). 1982 associate and in 1994 full academian member National Academy of Design, New York (today National Academy Museum and School). (PH)

Emmy van Leersum (16.04.1930 Hilversum, Niederlande – 02.11.1984 Amersfoort, Niederlande)
Schmuckkünstlerin. 1965 mit Gijs Bakker Schmuckatelier „De Werfkelder", Utrecht. 1970 Vorsitzende „Projectgroep Sieraden 1972 Binnenland". Lehrtätigkeit: 1975 Haystack Mountain School of Crafts, Deer Isle, Maine. 1982 mit Gijs Bakker Bezalel Academy, Jerusalem. Teilnahmen: 1968 Jablonec '68. II. Internationale Schmuckausstellung, Jablonec nad Nisou. 1970 Schmuck 70 – Tendenzen. Schmuckmuseum Pforzheim. 1971

Eröffnungsausstellung Electrum Gallery, London. 1972 Sieraad 1900–1972. Eerste Triennale. Zonnehof, Armersfoort. 1980 Schmuck International 1900–1980. Künstlerhaus Wien. Auszeichnungen: 1968 mit Gijs Bakker Gold- und Silbermedaille II. Internationale Schmuckausstellung, Jablonec nad Nisou. 1983 Herbert-Hofmann-Preis, Internationale Handwerksmesse München. I Studio jewelry artist. 1965 with Gijs Bakker jewelry atelier "De Werfkelder", Utrecht. 1970 Chairwoman "Projectgroep Sieraden 1972 Binnenland". Teaching: Haystack Mountain School of Crafts, Deer Isle, Maine. With Gijs Bakker Bezalel Academy, Jerusalem. Participations: 1968 Jablonec '68. II. International Jewelry Exhibition, Jablonec nad Nisou. 1970 Schmuck 70 – Tendenzen. Schmuckmuseum Pforzheim. 1971 opening exhibition Electrum Gallery, London. 1972 Sieraad 1900–1972. Eerste Triennale. Zonnehof, Armersfoort. 1980 Schmuck International 1900–1980. Künstlerhaus Vienna. Awards: 1968 with Gijs Bakker Gold- and Silver Medal II. International Jewelry Exhibition, Jablonec nad Nisou. 1983 Herbert Hofmann Award, Internationale Handwerksmesse München. (EL)

Robert Hedley Lewis (August 1925 – lebt in Cobham, Großbritannien)
1964 Mosaik für Londoner Untergrundbahn. 1992–1995 Direktor City and Guilds of London Art School und Direktor Byam Shaw School of Drawing & Painting, London. I 1964 Mosaic for London Underground. 1992–1995 Director City and Guilds of London Art School and of the Byam Shaw School of Drawing & Painting, London. (PH)

Vera List, geb. als Vera Glaser (1908 Brooklyn, MA, USA – 2002 Greenwich, CT, USA)
Mäzenin, Kunstsammlerin. 1962 Gründung Poster und Print Programm (Vera List Art Program). Lincoln Art Center, New York, Vorstandsmitglied Jewish Museum und American Federation of Arts. Auszeichnung: 1996 National Medal of Arts der USA. I Patroness, art collector. 1962 Founding of Poster and Print Program (Vera List Art Program). Lincoln Art Center, New York, Board of the Jewish Museum and the American Federation of Arts. Award: 1996 National Medal of Arts of the USA. (PH)

Tzaims Luksus (01.01.1932 Chicago, IL, USA – lebt und arbeitet in Bennington, VT, USA)
Künstler, Modedesigner. 1961 Philadelphia. Vorstellung von Grafikdrucken auf Seide. 1965 eigene Modekollektion. Eröffnet erstes amerikanisches Haute-Couture-Modehaus, New York. 1966 Bezeichnung als „New Christian Dior in fashion design". Weberei, Seidendruckerei und Designstudio in Bennington, 1968 als erster Amerikaner Modenschau in Paris. 1989 Gründung Vermont Foundation of Arts, Vermont Academy of Fine Arts, the Bennington Council on the Arts und 1995 Vermont Academy of Music, the Bennington Opera House. Lehrtätigkeit: Haystack Mountain School of Crafts, Deer Isle, Maine. Fashion Institute of Technology. Pratt Institute. Parsson School of Design, New York. Auszeichnungen: 1965 Neiman Marcus Award und Coty Award. 1974 Royal Society of Arts. I Artist, fashion designer. 1961 Philadelphia. Presentation of graphics on silk. 1965 first fashion collection. Launched the first major Fashion House in America, 1966 called the "New Christian Dior in fashion design". Own textile wool weaving mill and silk printing production and design studio, Bennington, 1968 first American fashion designer presenting a show in Paris. 1989 founds of Vermont Foundation of Arts, Vermont Academy of Fine Arts, the Bennington Council on the Arts and 1995 Vermont Academy of Music, the Bennington Opera House. Teaching: Haystack Mountain School of Crafts, Deer Isle, Maine. Fashion Institute of Technology. Pratt Institute. Parsson School of Design, New York. Awards: 1965 Neiman Marcus Award and Coty Award. 1974 Royal Society of Arts. (PH)

Fritz Maierhofer (02.02.1941 Wien, Österreich – lebt und arbeitet in Wien, Österreich)
Goldschmied, Entwerfer. 1965–1967 Werkstattleiter Anton Heldwein, Wien. 1969–1970 freischaffend, tätig bei Andrew Grima, London. 1971 Wien. Lehrtätigkeit: 1986–1987 Royal College of Art, London. Epsom College. 1989 Royal College of Art, London. 1991–1998 Schmuck-Workshops, Akademie Graz. Teilnahmen: 1971 Eröffnungsausstellung Electrum Gallery, London. 1973 Aspects of Jewellery. Aberdeen Art Gallery and Museum. 1975 Jewellery in Europe – An Exhibition of Progressive Work. The Scottish Arts Council Gallery, Edinburgh. u. a. (Wanderausst. bis 1977). 1980 Schmuck International 1900–1980. Künstlerhaus Wien. Auszeichnungen: 1972 Förderpreis des Wiener Kunstfonds, Wien. 1976 Stipendium des Ministeriums für Unterricht und Kunst, Wien. I Goldsmith, designer. 1965–1967 head of Atelier Heldwein, Vienna. 1969–1970 freelancer, working for Andrew Grima, London. Since 1971 Vienna. Teaching: 1986–1987 Royal College of Art, London. Epsom College. 1989 Royal College of Art, London. 1991–1998 Jewelry Workshops, Academy Graz. Participations: 1971 Opening Exhibition Electrum Gallery, Lon-

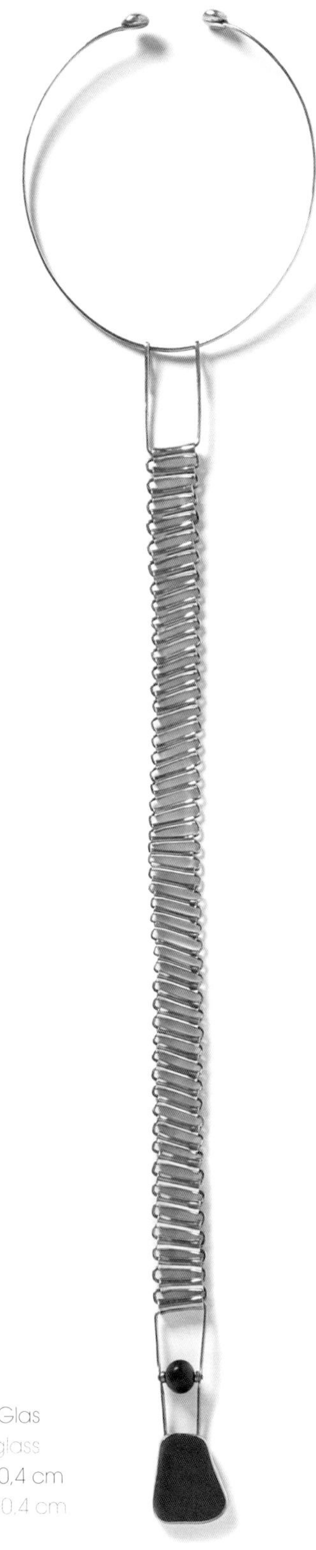

Halsschmuck
necklace,
1969/1971
Silber, Lapislazuli, Glas
silver, lapis lazuli, glass
H. 51 cm, B. 2,5–10,4 cm
h. 51 cm, w. 2,5–10,4 cm
Privatbesitz
private property

don. 1973 Aspects of Jewellery. Aberdeen Art Gallery and Museum. Jewellery in Europe – An Exhibition of Progressive Work. The Scottish Arts Council Gallery, Edinburgh et al. (touring. exh. til 1977). 1980 Schmuck International 1900–1980. Künstlerhaus Vienna. Awards: 1972 Förderpreis Wiener Kunstfonds, Vienna. 1976 Grant of the Ministerium für Unterricht und Kunst, Vienna. (EL)

Cherry Marshall, geb. als Irene Maud Pearson (25.07.1923, Christchurch, Großbritannien – 28.01.2006 Frinton-on-Sea, Großbritannien)
Model. Inhaberin Modelschule. 1938 Sängerin. 1939–1945 Armee-Kraftfahrerin. 1946 London-Hampstead. Haus wird Literatentreff. Ende 1940er-Jahre Model von und später Public Relation Manager bei Susan Smal. Anfrage Peter Zadeks als „Salome" für seine erste Inszenierung von Oskar Wildes „Salome". 1954–1974 Cherry Marshall Model Agency, Bond Street, London. Managed u. a. Vidal Sassoon, Patti Boyd, Suzi Kendall, Brenda Walker. 1956 Londoner Fashion-Show im Kaufhaus „Gum", Moskau. 1978 Publikation „Cat Walk". I Fashion model, model school. 1938 singer. 1939–1945 car driver in the army. 1946 London-Hampstead. Flat became meeting point for discussions on poetry and writing. End of the 1940s model and later public relation manager of Susan Smal. Peter Zadek asking her to be the "Salome" in his first Oscar Wilde "Salome" production. 1954–1974 Cherry Marshall Model Agency, Bond Street, London. Managing et al. Vidal Sassoon, Patti Boyd, Suzi Kendall, Brenda Walker. 1956 fashion show at department store "Gum", Moscow. 1978 publication "Cat Walk". (PH)

Bruno Martinazzi (10.12.1923 Turin – lebt und arbeitet in Turin, Italien)
Goldschmied, Bildhauer, Psychologe, Chemiker. Seit 1953 tätig als Bildhauer und Goldschmied. Lehrtätigkeit: 1965 Liceo Artistico, Turin. 1970 Gründung Sommer-Kunst-Schule, Ansedonia. 1976–1979 experimenteller Unterricht in Turin, Ansedonia, Mexiko und USA. Kunsttherapie an psychiatrischer Klinik, Turin-Collegno. Gründet Werkstätten für Kunst und Handwerk, Turin. 1976–1982 Accademia di Belle Arti, Turin. 1991–992 Royal College of Art, London. Teilnahmen: 1968 I. Internationales Symposium für Silberschmuck, Jablonec nad Nisou. 1970 Schmuck 70 – Tendenzen. Schmuckmuseum Pforzheim. 1971 Gold + Silber. Schmuck + Gerät von Albrecht Dürer bis zur Gegenwart. Norishalle, Nürnberg. 1971 Eröffnungsausstellung Electrum Gallery, London. 1975 Jewellery in Europe – An Exhibition of Progressive Work. The Scottish Arts Council Gallery, Edinburgh u. a. (Wanderausst. bis 1977). 1980 Schmuck International 1900–1980. Künstlerhaus Wien. 1991 20th Anniversary Electrum Gallery, London. Auszeichnungen: 1959 und 1961 Premio Gubbio I. Biennale del Metallo, Gubbio. 1961 Acquisition Award der „International Exhibition of Modern Jewellery", Goldsmith's Hall, London. 1964 Bayerischer Staatspreis Internationale Handwerksmesse München. I Goldsmith, sculptor, psychologist, chemist. Since 1953 working as sculptor and goldsmith. Teaching: 1965 Liceo Artistico, Turin. 1970 founded Summer Art School, Ansedonia. 1976–1979 experimental workshops in Turin, Ansedonia, Mexico and USA. Art therapy at psychiatric hospital, Torino-Collegno. Established first workshop for arts and crafts, Turin. 1976–1982 Academy of Fine Arts, Turin. 1991–1992 Royal College of

Art, London. Participations: 1968 I. International Symposium for Silver Jewellery, Jablonec nad Nisou. 1970 Schmuck 70 – Tendenzen. Schmuckmuseum Pforzheim. 1971 Gold + Silber. Schmuck + Gerät von Albrecht Dürer bis zur Gegenwart. Norishalle, Nuremberg. 1971 Opening Exhibition Electrum Gallery, London. 1975 Jewellery in Europe – An Exhibition of Progressive Work. The Scottish Arts Council Gallery, Edinburgh et al. (touring. exh. til 1977). 1980 Schmuck International 1900–1980. Künstlerhaus Vienna. 1991 20th Anniversary Electrum Gallery , London. Awards: 1959 and 1961 Premio Gubbio, I. Biennale del Metallo, Gubbio. 1961 Acquisition Award "International Exhibition of Modern Jewelery". Goldsmiths' Hall, London. 1964 Bayerischer Staatspreis Internation ale Handwerksmesse München. (EL)

Thomas Maria Messer (09.02.1920 Bratislava, Tschechoslowakei – 15.05.2013 New York, NY, USA)
Kunsthistoriker. 1945–1947 Mitarbeiter Office of U.S. Military Government, München. 1949–1952 Direktor Roswell Museum und Art Center. 1952–1956 American Federation of Arts: stellvertretender Direktor (1952–1953), verantwortlich für Ausstellungen (1953–1955), Direktor (1955–1956). 1957–1961 Direktor Institute of Contemporary Art, Boston. 1961–1988 Direktor und 1980–1988 Trustee Solomon R. Guggenheim Museum, New York. 1980 Direktor Peggy Guggenheim Collection, Venedig. I Art historian. 1945–1947 employee Office of U.S. Military Government, Munich. 1949–1952 Director Roswell Museum and Art Center. 1952–1956 American Federation of Arts: assistant director (1952–1953), director of exhibitions (1953–1955), director (1955–1956). 1957–1961 director Institute of Contemporary Art, Boston. 1961–1988 director and 1980–1988 trustee Solomon R. Guggenheim Museum, New York. 1980 director Peggy Guggenheim Collection, Venice. (PH)

Galerie PACE. London (1969–1971/1972)
Gegründet von Künstlerkooperative, u. a. Barbara Cartlidge. Nähe zu Friedens- und Frauenbewegung. Ausst.: 1969 Development of Modern Jewellery (u.a. Helga Zahn, Wendy Ramshaw) I Established by an artists cooperative, e. g. with Barbara Cartlidge. Close to the peace and women's movement. Exh.: 1969 Development of Modern Jewellery (Helga Zahn. Wendy Ramshaw, et al.). (PH)

Victor Pasmore (03.12.1908 Chelsham, England – 23.01.1998 Gudja, Malta)
Maler. 1927 Studio London. 1933 Mitglied Artists' Association, London. 1964 Beschäftigung mit Grafik. 1966 Malta. 1972 Video „The Image in Search of Itself". Lehrtätigkeit: 1943–1949 Leiter Bereich Malerei Camberwell School of Art. 1949 London County Council Central School of Arts and Crafts. 1953–1961 Leitung Malerei-Department King´s College. Durham University, Newcastle upon Tyne. Gründet „The Developing Process" (Studien in „Basic Form"). „Foundation Course", Sommerschule Scarborough. Teilnahmen: 1933 Association's Cooling Galleries, Bond Street, London. 1934 Objective Abstraction. 1948 Redfern Gallery. 1954 Retrospektive. Institute of Contemporary Arts, London und Arts Council Gallery, Cambridge. 1950/1951 erste Ausst. abstrakter Kunst in London nach dem Krieg. 1959 documenta 2. 1961 XXX. Biennale di Venezia. 1964 documenta 3 und 5. Internationale Kunstausstellung, Tokio. 1965 VII. Biennale São Paulo. 1965 Retrospektive. Tate Gallery, London. 1972 Grafik-Ausstellung, Rom. 1973 Paddington. Auszeichnungen: 1959 C.B.E. 1976 Grand Prix d'Honneur, International Graphik Biennale, Ljubljana. 1983 Royal Academy. Charles Wollaston Award. I Painter. 1927 studio London. 1933 member Artists' Association, London. 1964 working with graphics. 1966 Malta. 1972 Video "The Image in Search of Itself". Teaching: 1943–1949 Director of Painting, Camberwell School of Art, London. 1953–1961 head Department of Painting, King's College. Durham University, Newcastle upon Tyne. Established "The Developing Process" (studies in "Basic Form"). "Foundation Course", summer school Scaborough. Participations: 1933 Association's Cooling Galleries, Bond Street, London. 1934 Objective Abstraction. 1948 Redfern Gallery. 1954 Retrospective. Institute of Contemporary Arts, London and Arts Council Gallery, Cambridge. 1950/1951 first exhibition abstract painting in London after WW2. 1959 documenta 2. 1961 XXX. Biennale di Venezia. 1964 documenta 3 and 5. International Art Exhibition, Tokyo. 1965 VII. Biennale São Paulo. 1965 Retrospektive. Tate Gallery, London. 1972 Graphic exhibition, Rome. 1973 Paddington. Awards: 1959 C.B.E. 1976 Grand Prix d'Honneur, Ljubljana Biennale of Graphic Arts. 1983 elected Royal Academy. Charles Wollaston Award. (PH)

Ewan Maurice Godfrey van Zwanenberg Phillips (1914–1994)
Ewan Phillips Gallery (1964–1967/1968)
Kunsthistoriker, Kunsthändler. Mitbegründer Artists' Refugee Committee und Artist's International Foundation. 1938 Mitarbeit an Ausst. „German Art of the 20th Cen-

tury", London, als Gegenpol zur Ausst. „Entartete Kunst", München. 1939 Mitarbeiter Evakuierung National Gallery, London. Nach 1945 „Monument Man" in Hamburg und Schleswig-Holstein. 1948–1953 erster Direktor Institute for Contemporary Arts, London. Später Kunsthändler, spezialisiert in Post-Impressionismus und Moderne. 1964 Gründung Ewan Phillips Gallery, Maddox Street, London. Ralph Turner Assistent. Ausst. u.a. mit Helga Zahn (1965), Emmy van Leersum, Gijs Bakker. I Art historian, art dealer. Founding member Artists' Refugee Committee and Artist's International Foundation. 1938 worked on the exh. "German Art of the 20th Century", London, to counter exh. "Entartete Kunst", Munich. 1939 employee of evacuation National Gallery's, London. After 1945 "Monument Man" in Hamburg and Schleswig-Holstein. 1948–1953 first director of the newly formed Institute for Contemporary Arts, London. Later art dealer, specialized in Post-Impressionist and modernistic paintings. 1964 established Ewan Phillips Gallery, Maddox Street, London. Exh. Helga Zahn (1965), Emmy van Leersum, Gijs Bakker et al. Set Ralph Turner as assistent. (PH)

Mario Pinton (12.11.1919 Padua – 22.12.2008 Padua, Italien)
Gold-, Silberschmied, Graveur. 1954 Werkstatt Padua. Lehrtätigkeit: 1944–1969 Dozent Metall- und Goldschmiedekunst und 1969–1976 Direktor Istituto Statale d'Arte „Pietro Selvatico", Padua. 1976–1983 Direktor Istituto Superiore per le Industrie Artistiche, Urbino. 1983–1984 Leiter Istituto Statale d'Arte „M. Fanoli", Citadella. Teilnahmen: 1966 Internationale Handwerksmesse München. 1968 Jablonec '68. II. Internationale Schmuckausstellung, Jablonec nad Nisou. 1971 Gold + Silber. Schmuck + Gerät von Albrecht Dürer bis zur Gegenwart. Norishalle, Nürnberg. 1980 Schmuck International 1900–1980. Künstlerhaus Wien. Auszeichnungen: 1954 Bronzemedaille X. Triennale di Milano. 1957 Goldmedaille XI. Triennale di Milano. 1963 Biennale delle Arti Decorative, Venedig. 1964 Bayerischer Staatspreis Internationale Handwerksmesse München und Ministero dell Pubblica Istruzione, Vicenza. 1975 Goldener Ehrenring der Gesellschaft für Goldschmiedekunst, Hamburg. Herbert-Hofmann-Preis. Internationale Handwerksmesse München. Gold-, silversmith, engraver. 1954 studio Padua. Teaching: 1944–1969 lecturer metal- and goldsmithing and 1969–1976 director Istituto Statale d'Arte "Pietro Selvatico", Padua. 1976–1983 director Istituto Superiore per le Industrie Artistiche, Urbino. 1983–1984 director Istituto Statale d'Arte "M. Fanoli", Citadella. Participations: 1966 Internationale Handwerksmesse München. 1968 Jablonec '68. II. International Jewelry Exhibition, Jablonec nad Nisou. 1971 Gold + Silber. Schmuck + Gerät von Albrecht Dürer bis zur Gegenwart. Norishalle, Nuremberg. 1980 Schmuck International 1900–1980. Künstlerhaus Vienna. Awards: 1954 Bronze Medal X. Triennale di Milano. 1957 Gold Medal XI. Triennale di Milano. 1963 Biennale delle Arti Decorative, Venezia. 1964 Bayerischer Staatspreis Internationale Handwerksmesse München and Ministero dell Pubblica Istruzione, Vicenza. 1975 Goldener Ehrenring der Gesellschaft für Goldschmiedekunst, Hamburg. Herbert Hofmann Award, Internationale Handwerksmesse München. (EL)

Sidney Pizan
Mode- und Produktfotograf. Studio London-Hampstead. 1963 in BBC-Film „Cameras and cameramen". Fashion and product photographer. Studio London-Hampstead. 1963 in BBC film "Cameras and cameramen". (PH)

Queen Square Gallery. (1964 – 1978 Leeds, Großbtritannien)
1964 gegründet von Sarah Gilchrist in Leeds. 1968 Park Square. 1978 Pensionierung von Sarah Gilchrist. Ausst.: 1966 Weihnachtsausstellung (u. a. Barbara Cartlidge). 1969 New Jewellery. 1970 Weihnachtsausstellung – Glas. Skulptur und Schmuck (u. a. Wendy Ramshaw, Helga Zahn). 1971 Weihnachtsausstellung – Schmuck (u. a. Susanna Heron, Wendy Ramshaw, Helga Zahn). 1964 established by Sarah Gilchrist in Leeds. 1968 Park Square. 1978 retirement of Sarah Gilchrist. Exh.: 1966 Christmas Exhibition (Barbara Cartlidge et al.). 1969 New Jewellery. 1970 Christmas Exhibition – Glass, Sculpture and Jewellery (Wendy Ramshaw, Helga Zahn et al.). 1971 Christmas Exhibition – Jewellery (Susanna Heron, Wendy Ramshaw, Helga Zahn et al.). (PH)

Wendy Ramshaw (26.05.1939 Sunderland, Großbritannien – lebt in London, Großbritannien)
Schmuckkünstlerin, Autodidaktin. 1965 mit David Watkins und Pat Howard Gründung Modeschmuckfirma „Something Special". 1968 Werkstatt. 1973 Mitglied der Worshipful Company of Goldsmiths, London. Lehrtätigkeit: 1984 Bezalel Academy, Jerusalem und San Diego State University. 1996–1999 Royal College of Art, London. Teilnahmen: 1971 Gold + Silber. Schmuck + Gerät von Albrecht Dürer bis zur Gegenwart. Norishalle, Nürnberg. 1971 Eröffnungsausstellung Electrum Gallery, London. 1972 Sieraad 1900–1972. Eerste Triennale. Zonnehof, Armersfoort. 1973 The Craftsman's Art. Victoria & Albert Museum, London.

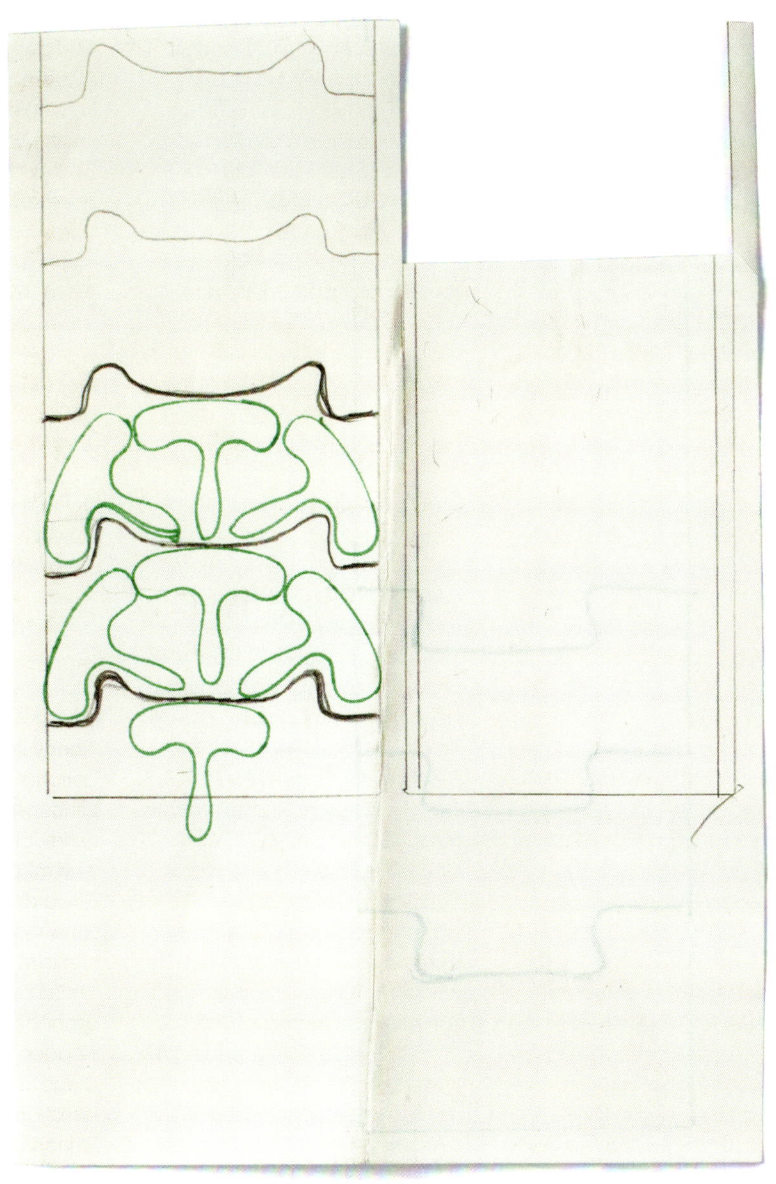

Entwurfszeichnungen für Anhänger | scetches for pendants, 1968/1971
Papier, Bleistift, Filzstift | paper, pencil, felt pen
H. 19,5 cm, B. 13,2 cm | h. 19,5 cm, w. 13,2 cm
Die Neue Sammlung – The Design Museum

1975 Jewellery in Europe – An Exhibition of Progressive Work. The Scottish Arts Council Gallery, Edinburgh u. a. (Wanderausst. bis 1977). 1980 Schmuck International 1900–1980. Künstlerhaus Wien. 1982 The Maker's Eye. Crafts Council Gallery, London. 1991 20th Anniversary Electrum Gallery, London. Auszeichnungen: 1970 De Beers Diamond Today. 1972 Council of Industrial Design, London. 1974 Johnson Matthey Award. World Crafts Council, Ontario. Crafts Advisory Committee Stipendium. 1975 De Beers Diamonds International Award, New York. 1983 Designers and Art Directors Association Award for Graphics. 1984 Forschungsstipendium Crafts Council, London. I Studio jewelry artist, autodidact. 1965 with David Watkins and Pat Howard founded fashion jewelry company "Something Special". 1968 studio. 1973 member of the Worshipful Company of Goldsmiths, London. Teaching: 1984 Bezalel Academy, Jerusalem and San Diego State University. 1996–1999 Royal College of Art, London.
Participations: 1971 Gold + Silber. Schmuck + Gerät von Albrecht Dürer bis zur Gegenwart. Norishalle, Nuremberg. 1971 Opening Exhibition Electrum Gallery, London. 1972 Sieraad 1900–1972. Eerste Triennale. Zonnehof, Armersfoort, Netherlands. 1973 The Craftsman's Art. Victoria & Albert Museum, London. 1975 Jewellery in Europe – An Exhibition of Progressive Work. The Scottish Arts Council Gallery, Edinburgh et al. (touring exh. til 1977). 1980 Schmuck International 1900–1980. Künstlerhaus Vienna. 1982 The Maker's Eye. Crafts Council Gallery, London. 1991 20th Anniversary Electrum Gallery, London. Awards: 1970 De Beers Diamond Today. 1972 Council of Industrial Design, Lodon. 1974 Johnson Matthey Award. World Crafts Council, Ontario. Crafts Advisory Committee Bursary. 1975 De Beers Diamonds International Award, New York. 1983 Designers and Art Directors Association Award for Graphics. 1984 research grant Crafts Council, London. (EL)

Reinhold Reiling (1922 Ersingen, Deutschland – 1983 Cranz, Schweiz)
Goldschmied. Lehrtätigkeit: 1953–1982 Staatliche Kunst- und Werkschule/Fachhochschule für Gestaltung, Pforzheim. 1969 Professor. Auszeichnungen: 1964 Bayerischer Staatspreis Internationale Handwerksmesse München
Goldsmith. Teaching: 1953–1982 Staatliche Kunst- und Werkschule/ Fachhochschule für Gestaltung, Pforzheim. 1969 professorship. Awards: 1964 Bayerischer Staatspreis Internationale Handwerksmesse München.

Paul Reilly (29.05.1912 Liverpool, Großbritannien – 11.10.1990)
Journalist, Betriebswirt. 1935 Mitarbeit bei Venesta und 1936 bei News Chronicle, London. 1946 bei Modern Plastics, New York, 1948 Großbritannien. Leiter Presse- und Öffentlichkeitsarbeit, 1957 stellvertretender und 1960–1977 Direktor Council of Industrial Design (seit 1972 Design Council). 1971–1977 Vorstandsvorsitzender Crafts Advisory Committee, London. Vorsitzender Conran Foundation, London. 1982 Entwicklung Boilerhouse Project, Victoria & Albert Museum, London, und Design Museum London (eröffnet 1987). Auszeichnungen: 1961 Kommandeur des Wasaorden. 1965 Royal Institute of British Architects. 1967 Knight Bachelor. 1978 Life Peer Act und Erhebung zum Baron Reilly of Brompton. 1978 Royal Borough of Kensington and Chelsea. Ehrendoktorwürden: 1977 Loughborough University, Leicestershire. 1978 Royal College of Art, London. 1981 Aston University, Birmingham. 1983 Cranfield University. I Journalist, economist. 1935 employment at Venesta and 1936 at New Chronicle, London. 1946 at Modern Plastics, New York, NY. 1948 Great Britain. Chief information officer, 1957 deputy director and 1960–1977 director Council of Industrial Design (since 1972 Design Council). 1971–1977 chief executive Crafts Advisory Committee, London. Chairman Conran Foundation, London. 1982 developing Boilerhouse Project at Victoria & Albert Museum, London, and at Design Museum London (opened 1987). Awards: 1961 Commander of the Order of Wasa. 1965 Royal Institute of British Architects. 1967 Knight Bachelor. 1978 Life Peer Act and ennobled Baron Reilly. 1978 Royal Borough of Kensington and Chelsea. Honorary doctorates: 1977 Loughborough University, Leicestershire. 1978 Royal College of Art, London. 1981 Aston University, Birmingham. 1983 Cranfield University. (EL)

Franz Rickert (09.01.1904 Freiburg, Deutschland – 01.01.1991 München, Deutschland)
Gold-, Silberschmied. 1925 Werkstatt München. 1933 Schriftführer Bayerischer Kunstgewerbeverein. Lehrtätigkeit: 1935–1972 Leiter Klasse für Metall- und Goldschmiedekunst (später: Klasse für Gold- und Silberschmiedekunst) an Staatsschule für Angewandte Kunst Müchen (ehem. Kunstgewerbeschule). 1938 außerordentlicher Professor. Teilnahmen: 1971 Gold + Silber. Schmuck + Gerät von Albrecht Dürer bis zur Gegenwart. Norishalle, Nürnberg. 1959–1984 Internationale Handwerksmesse München. Auszeichnungen: 1933 Ehrenring Gesellschaft für Goldschmiedekunst, Berlin. 1963 Ehrenpreis Bayerische Akademie der

Schönen Künste. 1973 Bundesverdienstkreuz. 1984 Bayerischer Verdienstorden. I Gold-, silversmith. 1925 studio in Munich. 1933 clerk at Bayerischer Kunstgewerbeverein. Teaching: 1935–1972 head metalsmith and goldsmith class (later: class for gold- and silversmith's work), Staatsschule für Angewandte Kunst Munich (formerly Kunstgewerbeschule). 1938 associate professor. Participations: 1971 Gold + Silber. Schmuck + Gerät von Albrecht Dürer bis zur Gegenwart. Norishalle, Nuremberg. 1984 Schmuck und Gerät 1959–1984 Internationale Handwerksmesse München. Awards: 1933 Ehrenring der Gesellschaft für Goldschmiedekunst, Berlin. 1963 Award of Bayerische Akademie der Schönen Künste. 1973 Bundesverdienstkreuz. 1984 Bayerischer Verdienstorden. (EL)

Harry Thubron (1915 Bishop Auckland, Großbritannien – 1985 London, Großbritannien)
Künstler, Kunstlehrer. Lehrtätigkeit: 1950–1955 Sunderland College of Art. 1955–1964 Leiter Abteilung für bildende Kunst, Leeds College of Art. 1971 Goldsmiths College New Cross, London (heute Goldsmiths, University of London). Teilnahmen: 1967 Queen Square Gallery, London. 1974 British Art. Hayward Gallery, London. 1977 British Painting 1952–1977. Royal Academy, London. I Artist, art teacher. Teaching: 1950–1955 Sunderland College of Art. 1955–1964 director department of art. Leeds College of Art. 1971 Goldsmiths College New Cross, London (today Goldsmiths, University of London). Participations: 1967 Queen Square Gallery, London. 1974 British Art. Hayward Gallery, London. 1977 British Painting 1952–1977. Royal Academy, London. (MS)

Ralph Turner
Kurator, Autor, Spezialist für Keramik und Schmuck. 1960er-Jahre Assistent in Ewan Phillips Galerie, London. 1971 mit Barbara Cartlidge Gründung der Electrum Galerie, London. 1971–1974 Galeriedirektor. 1974–1989 Ausstellungsleiter Crafts Council, London. Ausst.: 1975 Jewellery in Europe. An exhibition of progressive Work, Edinburgh u. a. (Wanderausst. bis 1977). 1975–1976 On Tour: 10 British Jewellers in Germany and Australia, Duisburg u.a. 1976 Helga Zahn. A Retrospective Assessment 1960–1976. Jewellery, Prints and Drawings, Crafts Advisory Committee, London. 1983 New Departures in British Jewellery, London. I Curator, author, specialized in ceramics and jewelry. During 1960s assistant at Ewan Phillips Gallery. 1971 founded with Barbara Cartlidge Electrum Gallery, London. 1971–1974 director of the gallery. 1974–1989 head of Exhibition at Crafts Council, London. Exh.: Jewellery in Europe. An exhibition of progressive Work. Edinburgh et al. (touring exh. til 1977). 1975-1976 On Tour: 10 British Jewellers in Germany and Australia. Duisburg et. al. 1976 Helga Zahn. A Retrospective Assessment 1960–1976. Jewellery, Prints, Drawings, Crafts Advisory Committee, London. 1983 New Departures in British Jewellery. London. (MS)

Klaus Ullrich (1927 Sensburg, Deutschland – 1998 Pforzheim, Deutschland)
Gold-, Silberschmied. Lehrtätigkeit: 1957 Dozent für Schmuckgestaltung, Kunst + Werkschule, Pforzheim (später Fachhochschule für Gestaltung, heute Hochschule Pforzheim). 1969–1989 Professur. Teilnahmen: 1966 Internationale Handwerksmesse München. 1970 Schmuck 70 – Tendenzen. Schmuckmuseum Pforzheim. 1971 Gold + Silber. Schmuck + Gerät von Albrecht Dürer bis zur Gegenwart. Norishalle, Nürnberg. Auszeichnungen: 1961 Staatspreis Baden-Württemberg. 1963 Bayerischer Staatspreis Internationale Handwerksmesse München. 1964 Goldmedaille für Schmuck. XIII. Triennale di Milano. 1976 Silbermedaille für Schmuck, Celje (Jugoslawien). I Gold-, silversmith. Teaching: 1957 instructor for jewelry, Kunst + Werkschule, Pforzheim (later Fachhochschule für Gestaltung, today Hochschule Pforzheim). 1969–1989 professor. Participations: 1966 Internationale Handwerksmesse München. 1970 Schmuck 70 – Tendenzen. Schmuckmuseum Pforzheim. 1971 Gold + Silber. Schmuck + Gerät von Albrecht Dürer bis zur Gegenwart. Norishalle, Nuremberg. Awards: 1961 Staatspreis Baden-Württemberg. 1963 Bayerischer Staatspreis Internationale Handwerksmesse München. 1964 Gold Medal for jewelry. XIII. Triennale di Milano. 1976 Silver Medal for jewelry, Celje (Yugoslavia). (EL)

David Watkins
(14.11.1940 Wolverhampton, Großbritannien – lebt und arbeitet in London, Großbritannien)
Schmuckkünstler, Bildhauer. 1963–1967 tätig als Bildhauer, Jazz- und Bluesmusiker. 1965 mit Wendy Ramshaw und Pat Howard Gründung der Modeschmuckfirma „Something Special". Seit 1966 Modellbauer für Filmindustrie. Lehrtätigkeit: 1963–1965 Kunstlehrer. Gastdozent für 3-D Design. 1984 Bezalel Academy, Jerusalem. 1984–2006 Professor und Leiter Department für Gold- und Silberschmieden, Metallgestaltung und Schmuck und 2006–2008 Professor für Schmuckforschung und Direktor des Zentrums für Schmuckforschung, Royal College of Art,

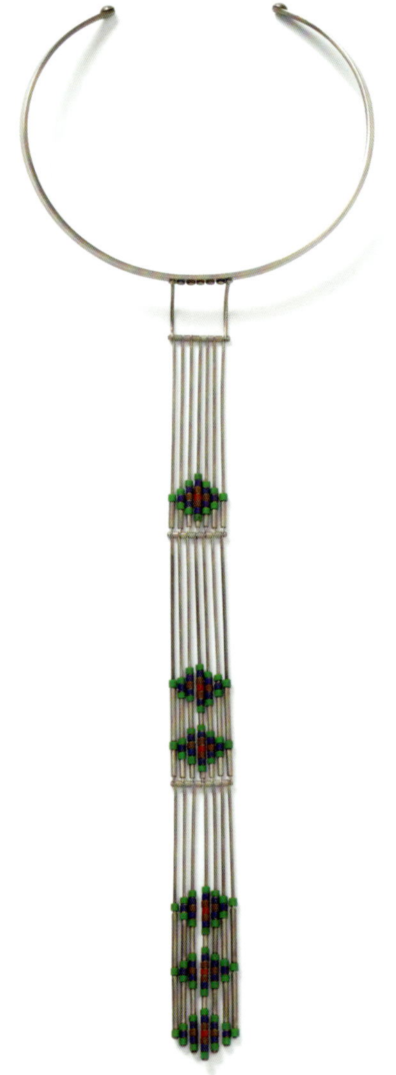

Halsschmuck | necklace, 1975–1978
Silber, Perlen | silver, beads
H. 40 cm, B. 2,4–13,5 cm | h. 40 cm, w. 2,4–13,5 cm
Privatbesitz | private property

London. Teilnahmen: 1971 Eröffnungs- ausstellung Electrum Gallery, London. 1975 Jewellery in Europe – An Exhibition of Progressive Work. The Scottish Arts Council Gallery, Edinburgh u. a. (Wanderausst. bis 1977). 1980 Schmuck International 1900–1980. Künstlerhaus Wien. 1982 The Maker's Eye. Crafts Council Gallery, London | Studio jewelry artist, sculptor. 1963–1967 worked as sculptor, Jazz and Blues musician. 1965 with Wendy Ramshaw and Pat Howard founding of the fash- ion jewelry company "Something Special". Teaching: 1963–1965 art teacher. Guest lecturer in 3-D design. 1984 Bezalel Academy, Jerusalem. 1984–2006 professor and head of gold- and silversmithing, metalwork and jewelry and 2006–2008 research professor and director at Centre for Jewelry Re-sesarch, Royal College of Art, London. Participations: 1971 Opening Exhibition Electrum Gallery, London. 1975 Jewellery in Europe – An Exhibition of Progressive Work. The Scottish Arts Council Gallery, Edinburgh et al. (touring exh. til 1977). 1980 Schmuck International 1900 – 1980. Künstlerhaus Vienna. 1982 The Maker's Eye. Crafts Council Gallery, London. (EL)

James Noel White
Lehrtätigkeit: Cambridge Universität. 1960 stellvertretender Direktor Council of Industrial Design, London. 1966 Repräsentant und 1968 Europäischer Vizepräsident World Crafts Council. 1973–1981 Vorsitzender des Crafts Study Center, Bath. Ehrenmitglied World Crafts Council. United Kingdom | Teaching: Cambridge University. 1960 Deputy Director. Council of Industrial Design, London. 1966 representative and 1968 European Vice-President of the World Crafts Council. 1973–1981 Chairman of the Crafts Study Center, Bath. Honorary Member. World Crafts Council, Great Britain. (EL)

Die Viten orientieren sich an den Lebensdaten von Helga Zahn
The vitae are based on the dates of Helga Zahn's life.

"Helga Zahn's work was 'soft' modernistic, without pretention, clear, sensual and human. In the Netherlands completely different things were going on. Renewal which was extremely interesting, but also drifted the jewelry away from the user, the physical, psychological and social person. Realising this, I try now, to restore the connection with the human in my choice for Galerie Ra and in my own jewellery-production. In this light I appreciate the work by Helga Zahn more and more and see her now as an important pioneer and artist."

Paul Derrez, Schmuckkünstler, Direktor Galerie Ra [3]

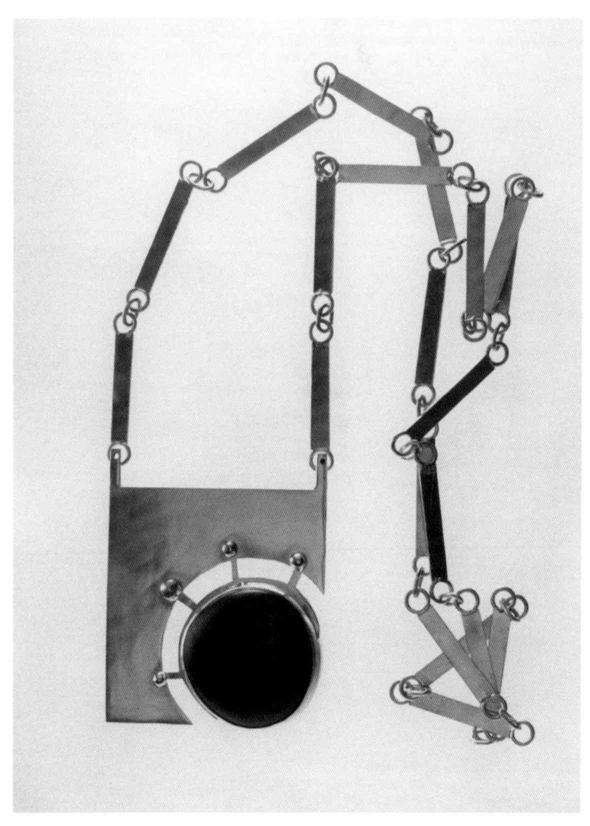

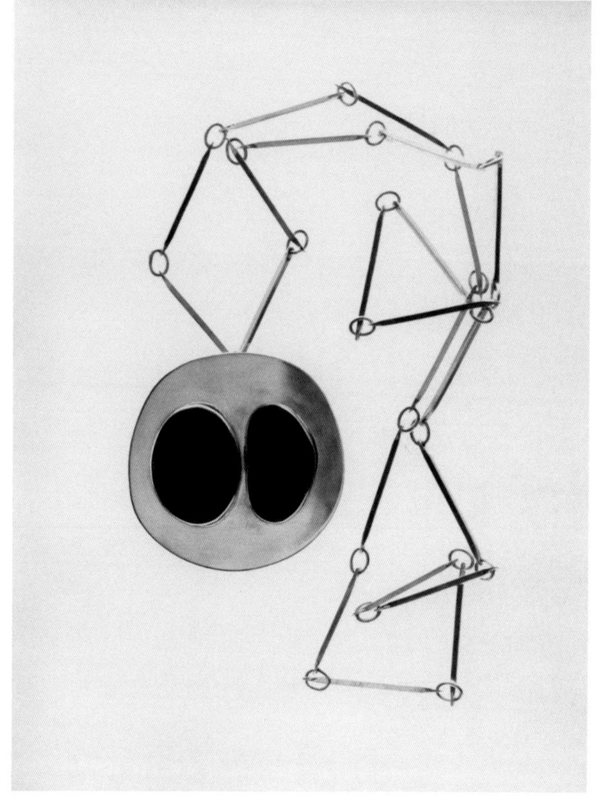

Tessa Grimshaw, ca. 1961
Halsschmuck von Helga Zahn | necklace by Helga Zahn
Foto: Archiv Helga Zahn

Tessa Grimshaw, ca. 1961
Halsschmuck von Helga Zahn | necklace by Helga Zahn
Foto: Archiv Helga Zahn

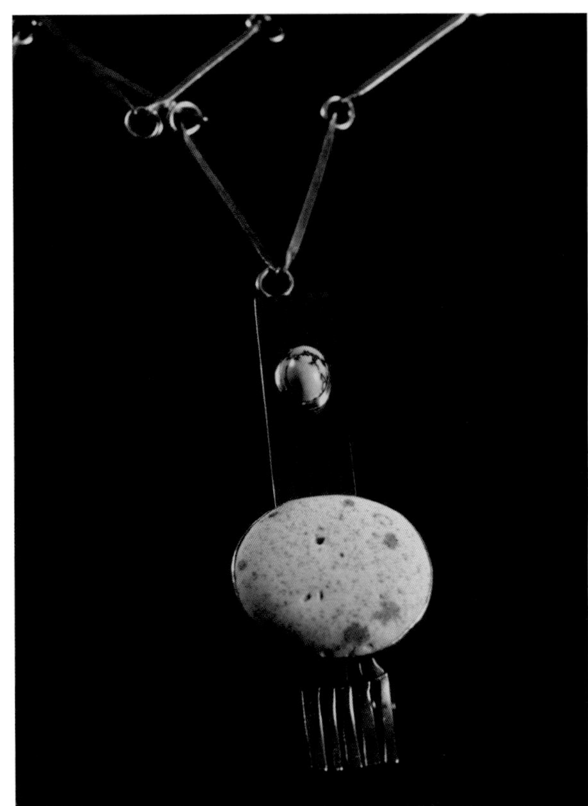

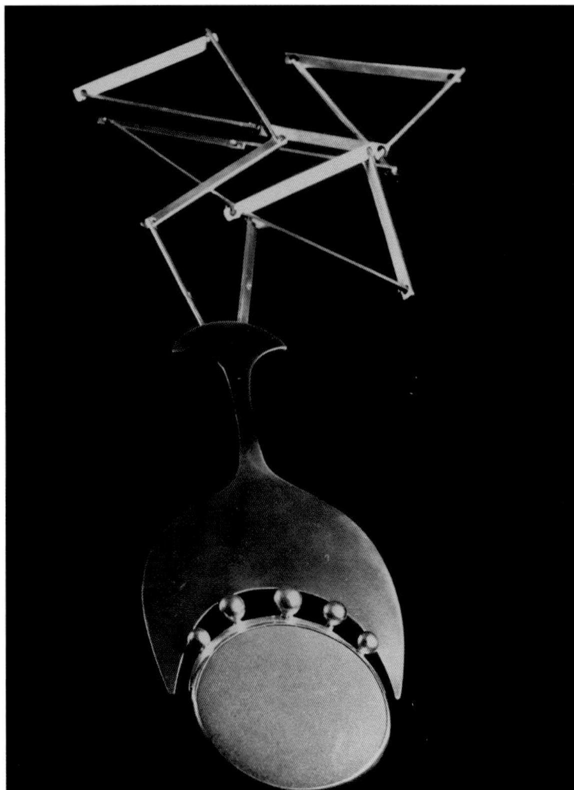

Sidney Pizan, ca. 1961
Halsschmuck von Helga Zahn | necklace by Helga Zahn
Foto: Archiv Helga Zahn

Sidney Pizan, ca. 1961
Halsschmuck von Helga Zahn | necklace by Helga Zahn
Foto: Archiv Helga Zahn

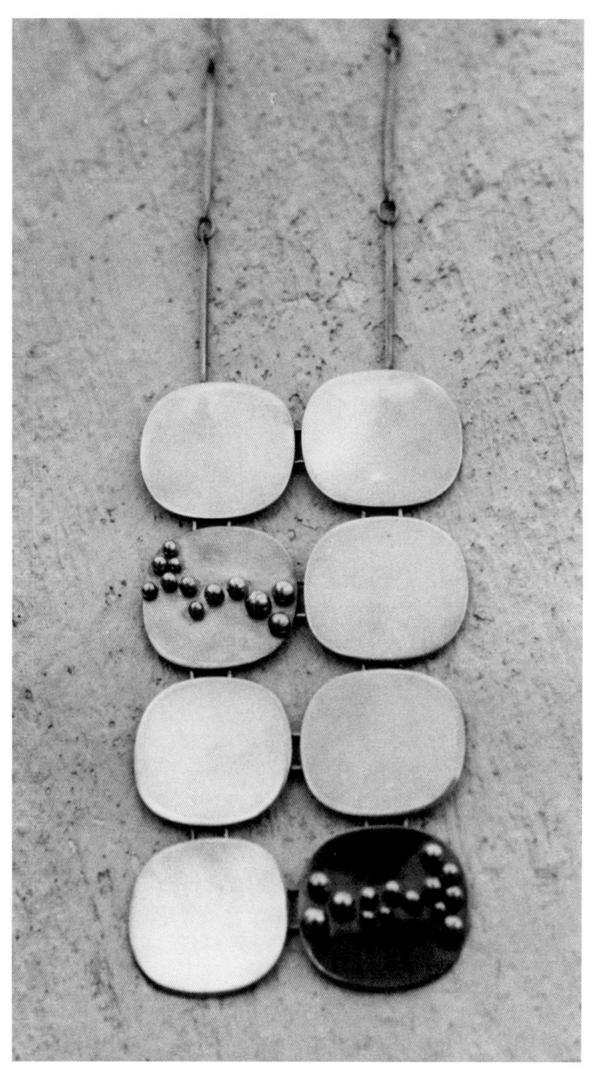

Unbekannter Fotograf | unknown photographer
Anhänger von Helga Zahn | pendant by Helga Zahn, 1965
Foto: Archiv Helga Zahn

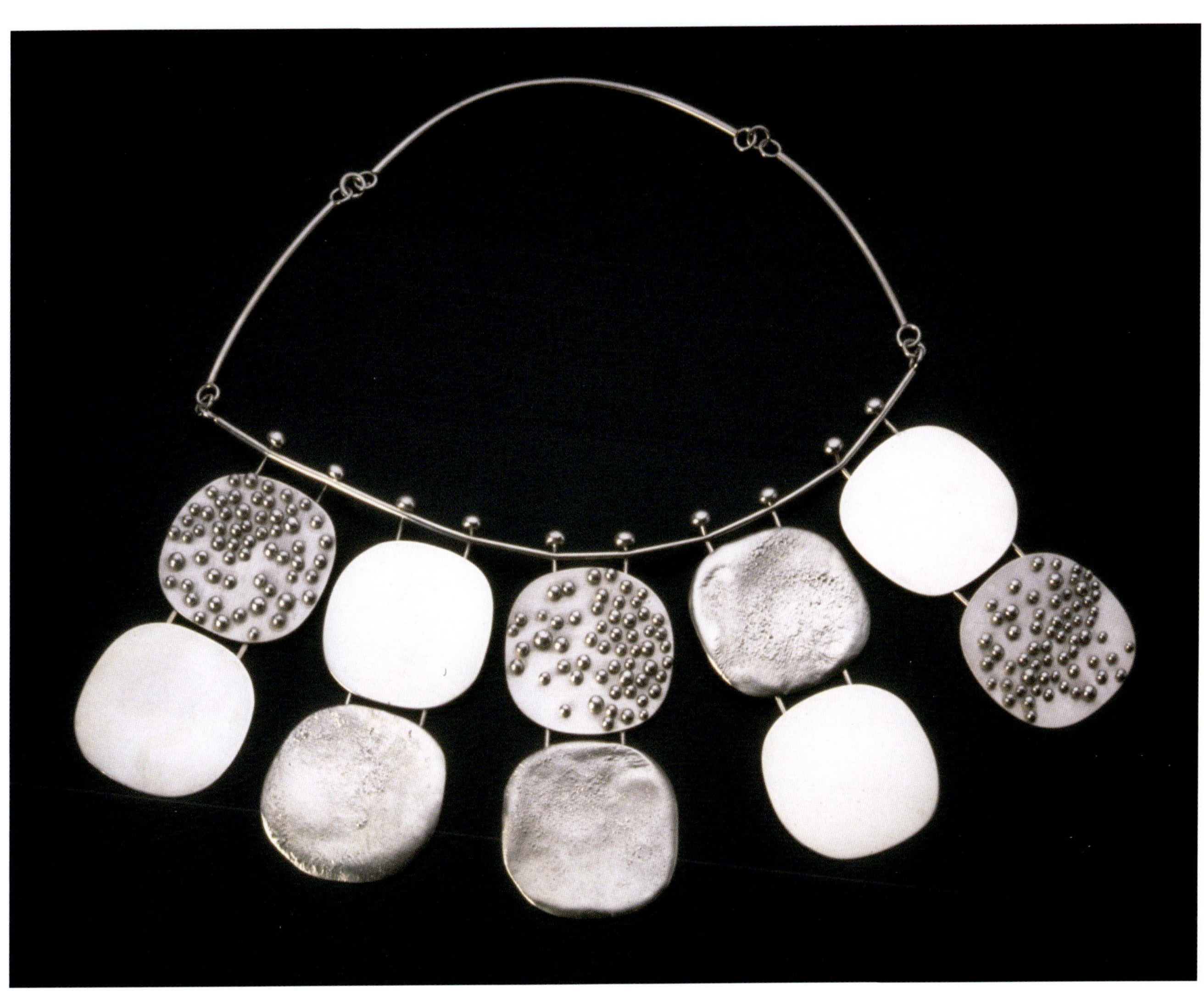

Unbekannter Fotograf | unknown photographer
Halsschmuck von Helga Zahn | necklace by Helga Zahn, 1965
Silber | silver
H. 25,2 cm, B. 28 cm | h. 25,2 cm, w. 28 cm
Foto: Archiv Helga Zahn

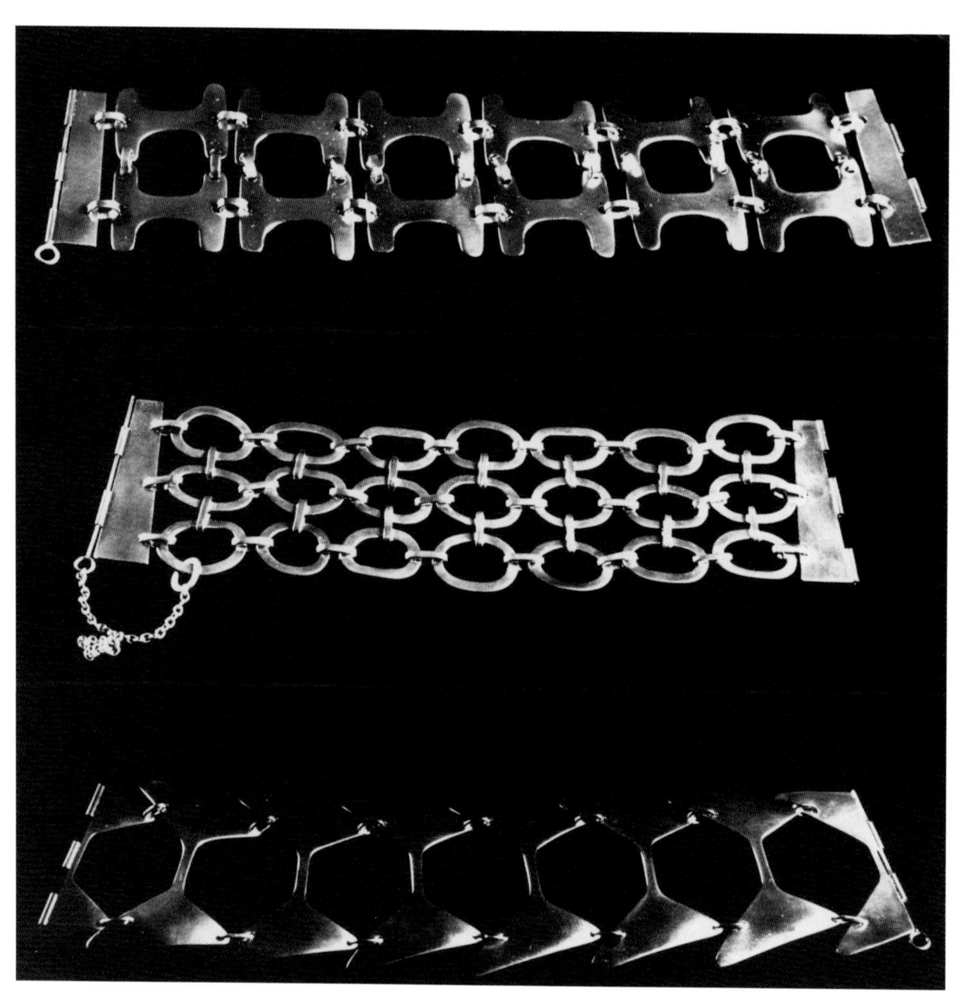

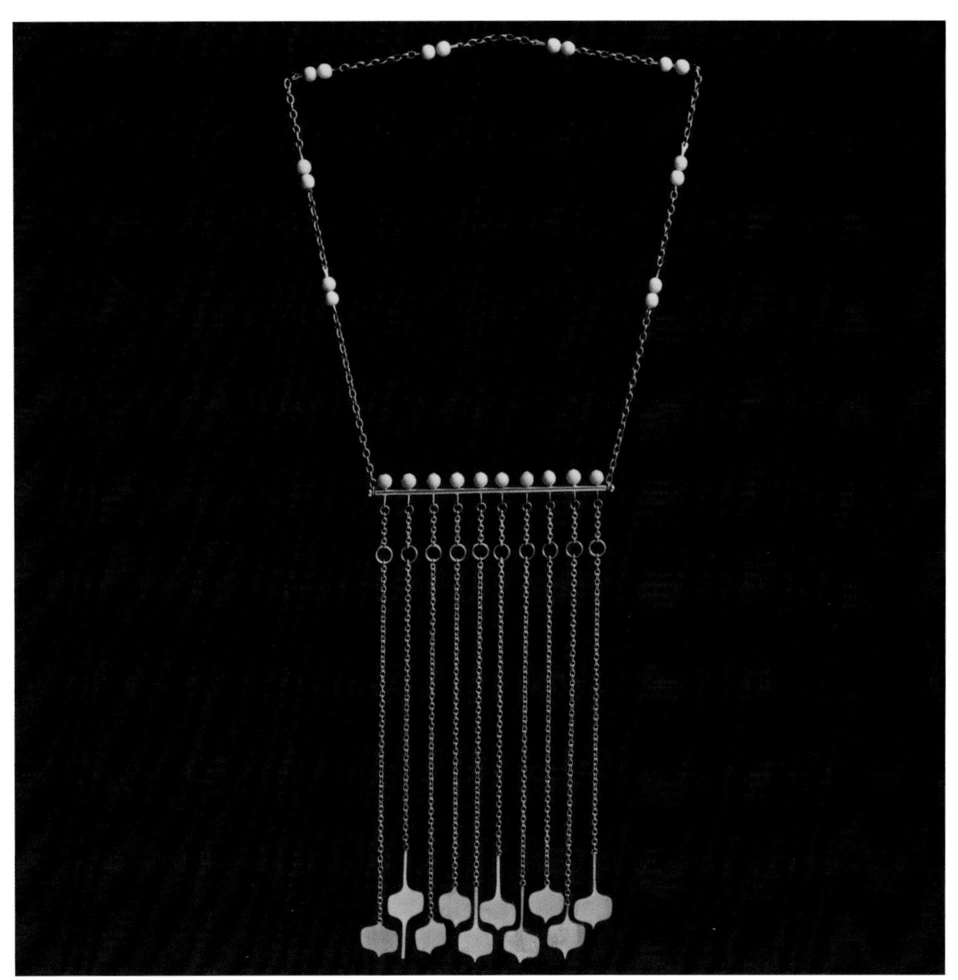

Unbekannter Fotograf | unknown photographer
Armschmuck von Helga Zahn | bracelets by Helga Zahn
Foto: Archiv Helga Zahn

Unbekannter Fotograf | unknown photographer
Halsschmuck von Helga Zahn | necklace by Helga Zahn, 1969 (?)
Gold, Silber, Elfenbeinperlen | gold, silver, ivory beads
Wendy Ramshaw
Foto: Archiv Helga Zahn

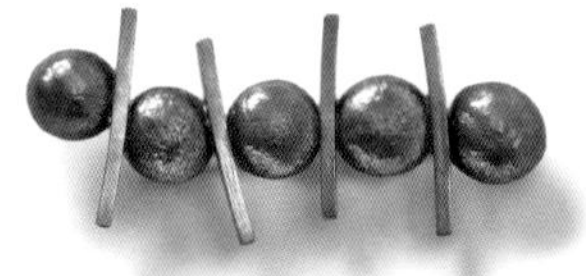

Brosche | brooch, 1962
Silber | silver
H. 2 cm, B. 5 cm | h. 2 cm, w. 5 cm
Privatbesitz | private property

Anhänger | pendant, 1962
Silber | silver
H. 4,7 cm, B. 10,2 cm | h. 4,7 cm, w. 10,2 cm
Privatbesitz | private property

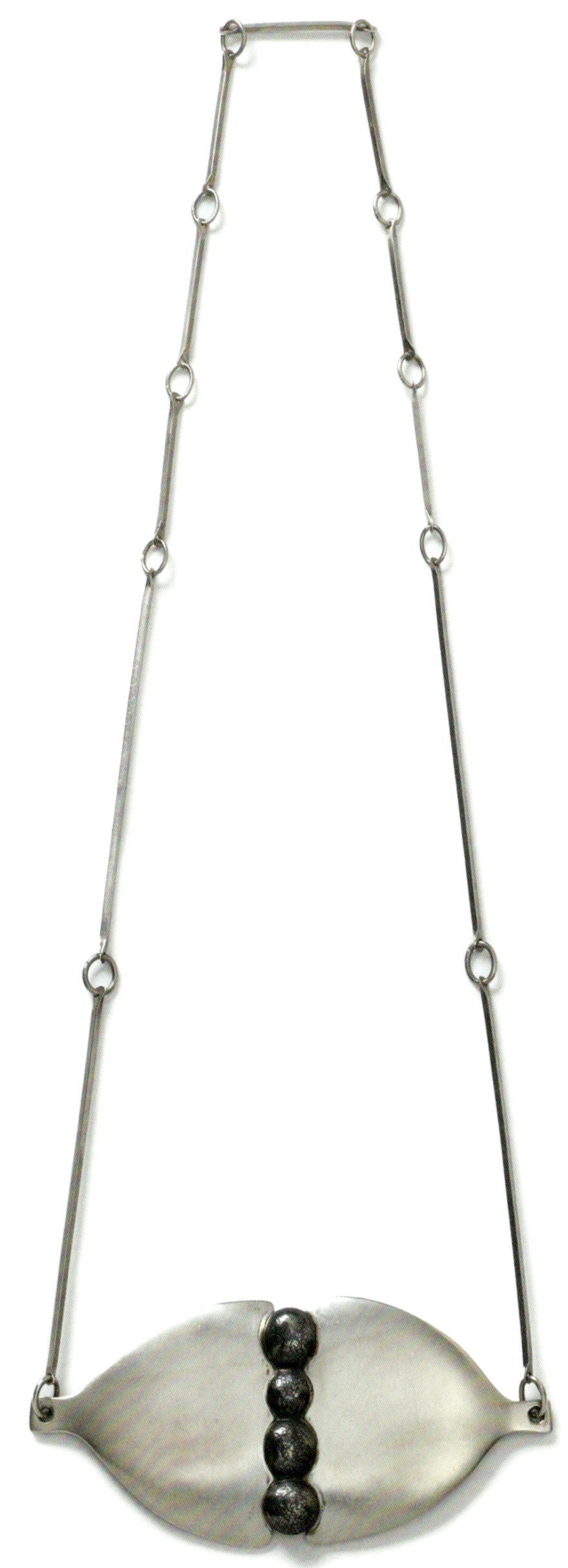

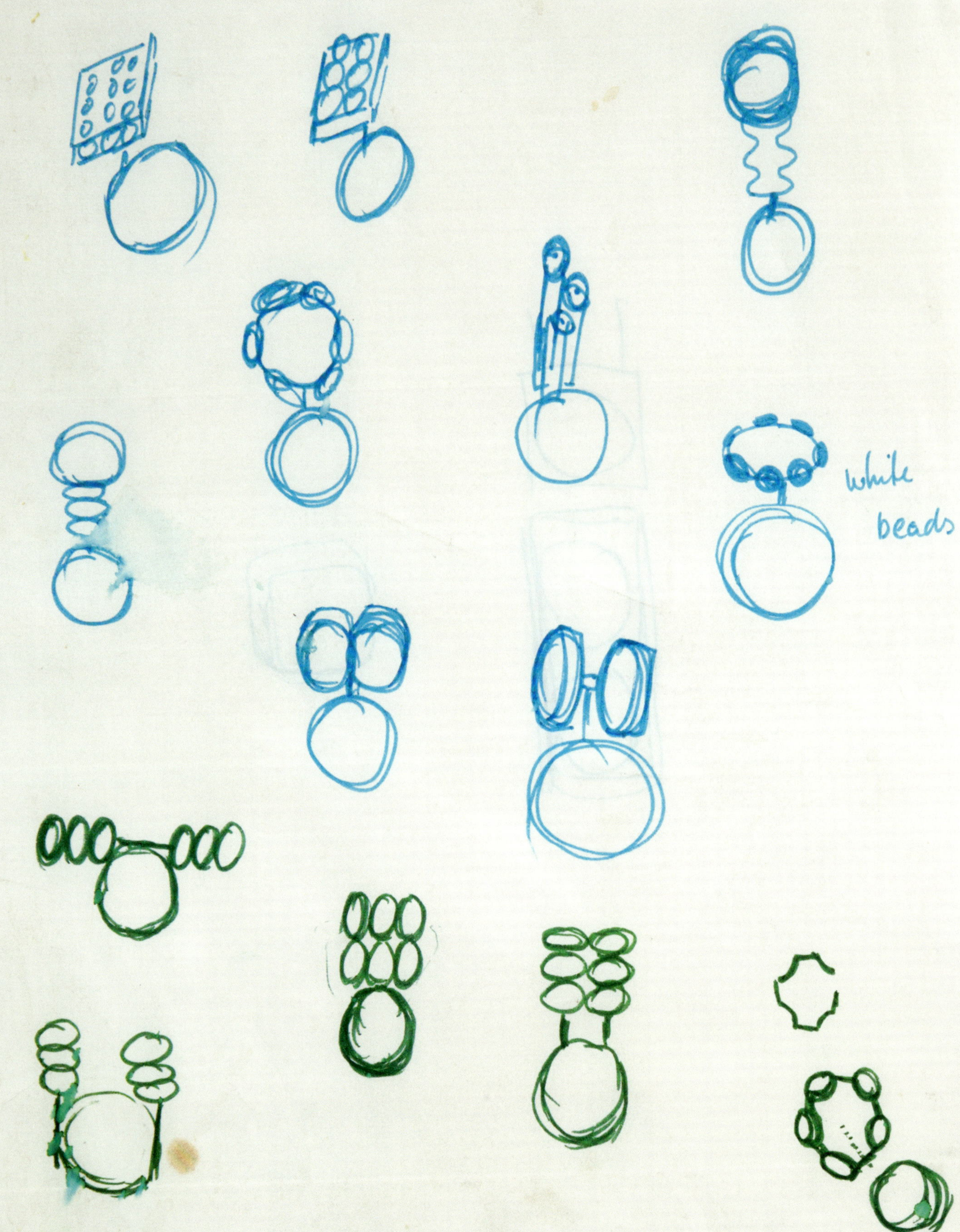
white
beads

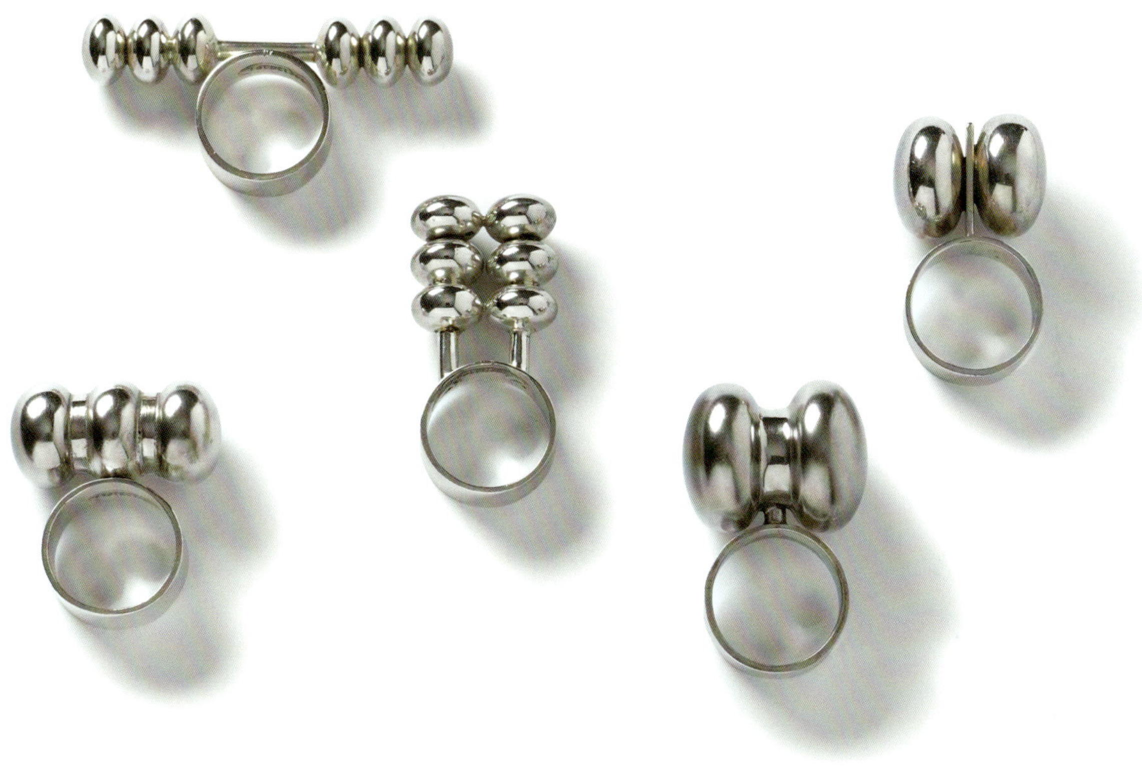

Entwürfe für Ringe | scetches for rings, 1968
Papier, Filzstift | paper, felt pen
H. 27,7 cm, B. 21,5 cm | h. 27,7 cm, w. 21,5 cm
Die Neue Sammlung – The Design Museum

Ringe | rings, 1967–1969
Silber | silver
H. 2,6–4,5 cm, B. 2–5,5 cm | h. 2,6–4,5 cm, w. 2–5,5 cm
Privatbesitz und Die Neue Sammlung – The Design Museum.Dauerleihgabe der Danner-Stiftung München | private property and Die Neue Sammlung – The Design Museum. Permanent loan of the Danner Foundation Munich

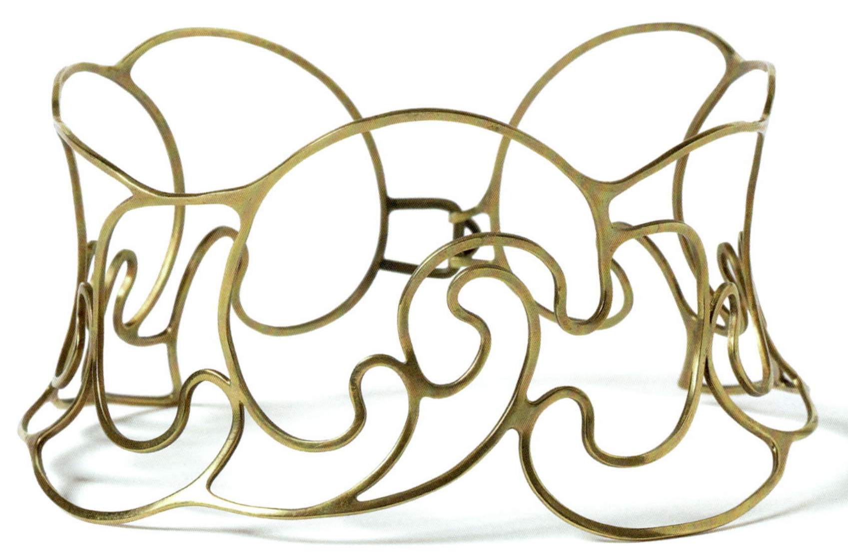

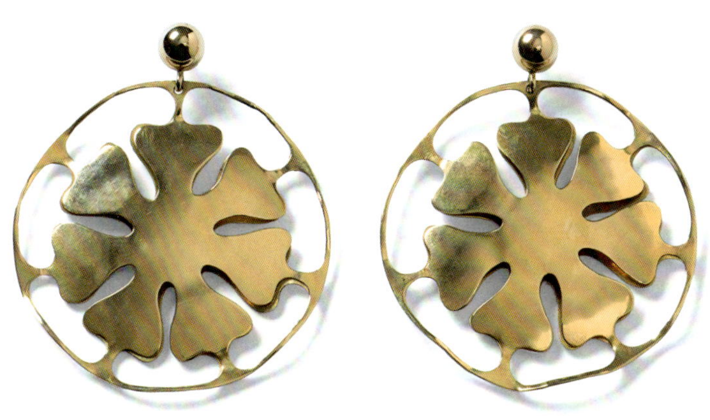

Halsschmuck | necklace, 1970 (?)
Gold | gold
H. 5,7 cm, Dm. 11,5 cm | h. 5,7 cm, diam. 11,5 cm
Privatbesitz | private property

Ohrschmuck | earrings, 1967
Gold | gold
Dm. 5,5 cm | diam. 5,5 cm
Privatbesitz | private property

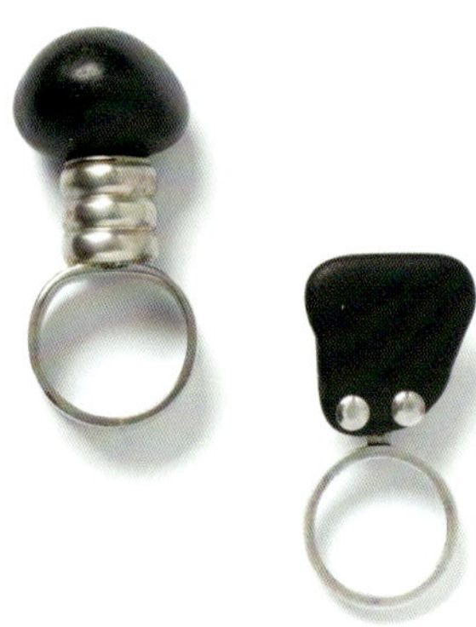

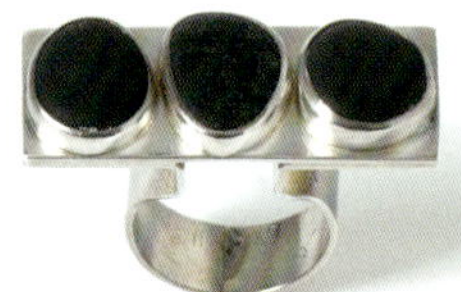

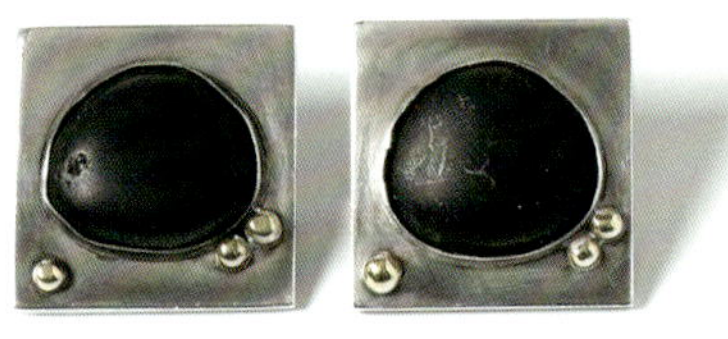

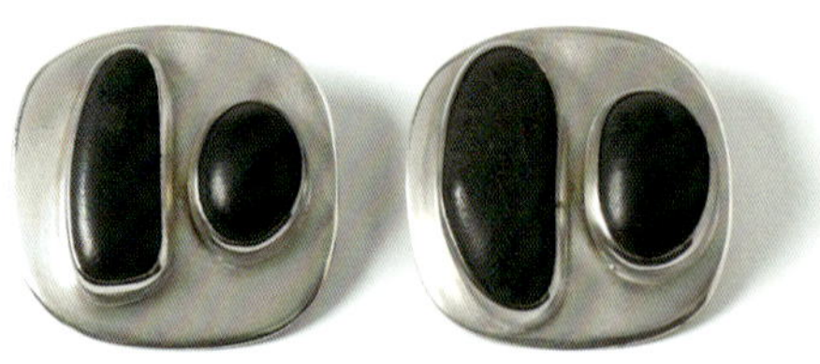

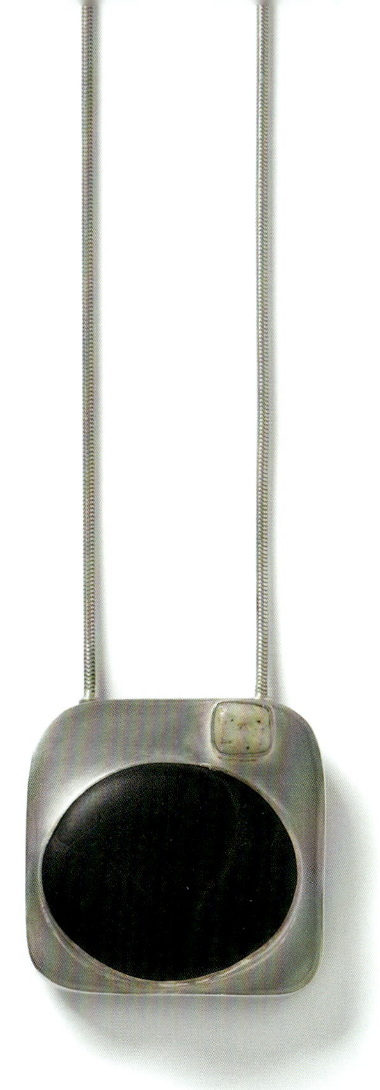

Ringe | rings, 1968
Silber, Kieselsteine | silver, pebble stones
H. 4–4,7 cm, B. 2,1–2,5 cm | h. 4–4,7 cm, w. 2,1–2,5 cm
Privatbesitz | private property

Ring und Manschettenknöpfe | ring and cufflinks, 1962
Silber, Kieselsteine | silver, pebble stones
Ring: Dm. 1,4 cm | ring: diam. 1,4 cm
Manschettenknöpfe: H. 2,3–2,8 cm, B. 2,4–3 cm | cufflinks: h. 2,3–2,8 cm, w. 2,4–3 cm
Privatbesitz | private property

Anhänger | pendant, 1961 (?)
Silber, Kieselsteine | silver, pebble stones
H. 6 cm, B. 6 cm, T. 1,6 cm | h. 6 cm, w. 6 cm, d. 1,6 cm
Privatbesitz | private property

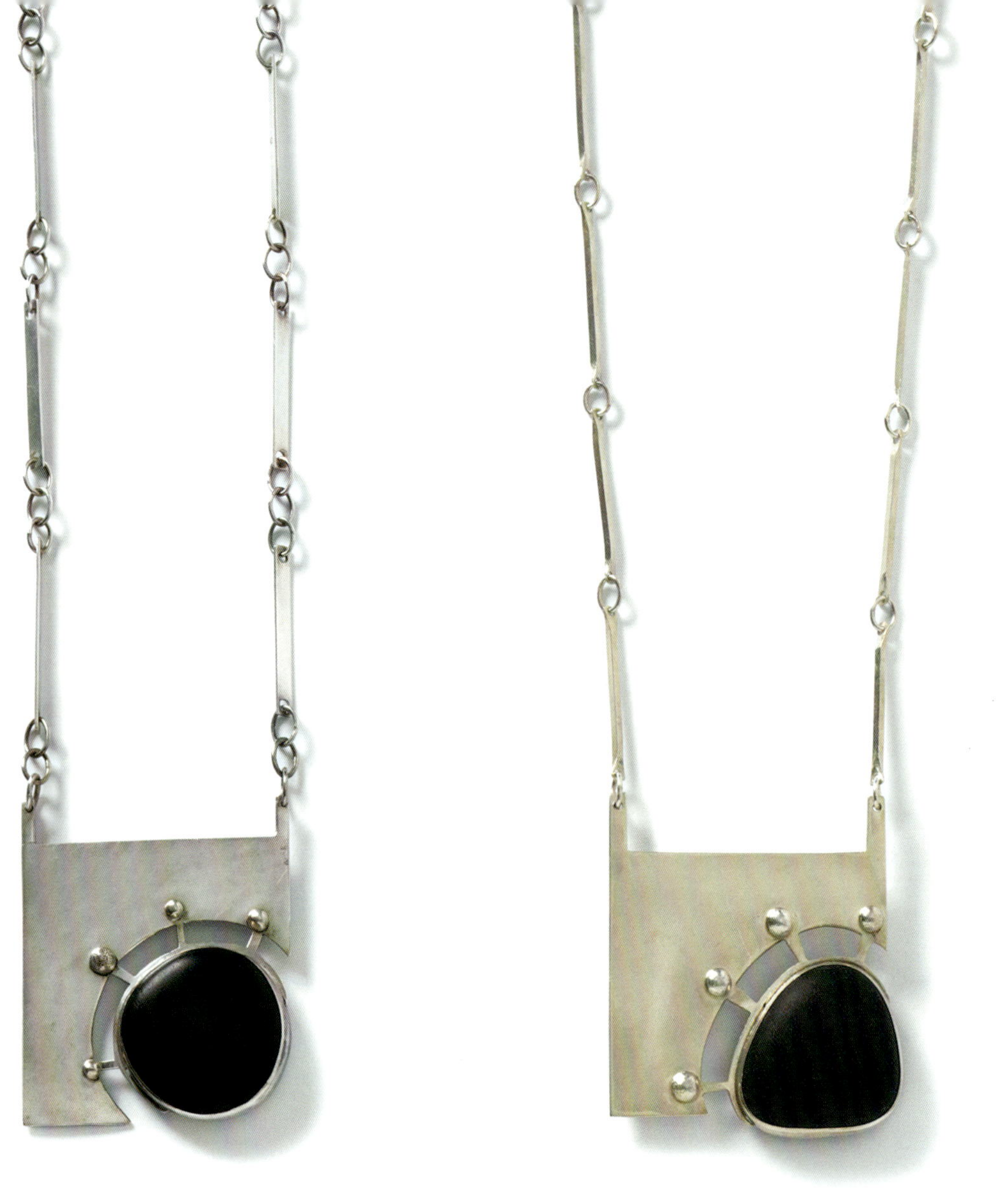

Halsschmuck | necklace, 1961
Silber, Kieselsteine | silver, pebble stones
H. 6 cm, B. 5 cm | h. 6 cm, w. 5 cm
Privatbesitz | private property

Halsschmuck | necklace, 1961
Silber, Kieselsteine | silver, pebble stones
H. 5,7 cm, B. 5,3 cm | h. 5,7 cm, w. 5,3 cm
Privatbesitz Monika Dölling | private property Monika Dölling

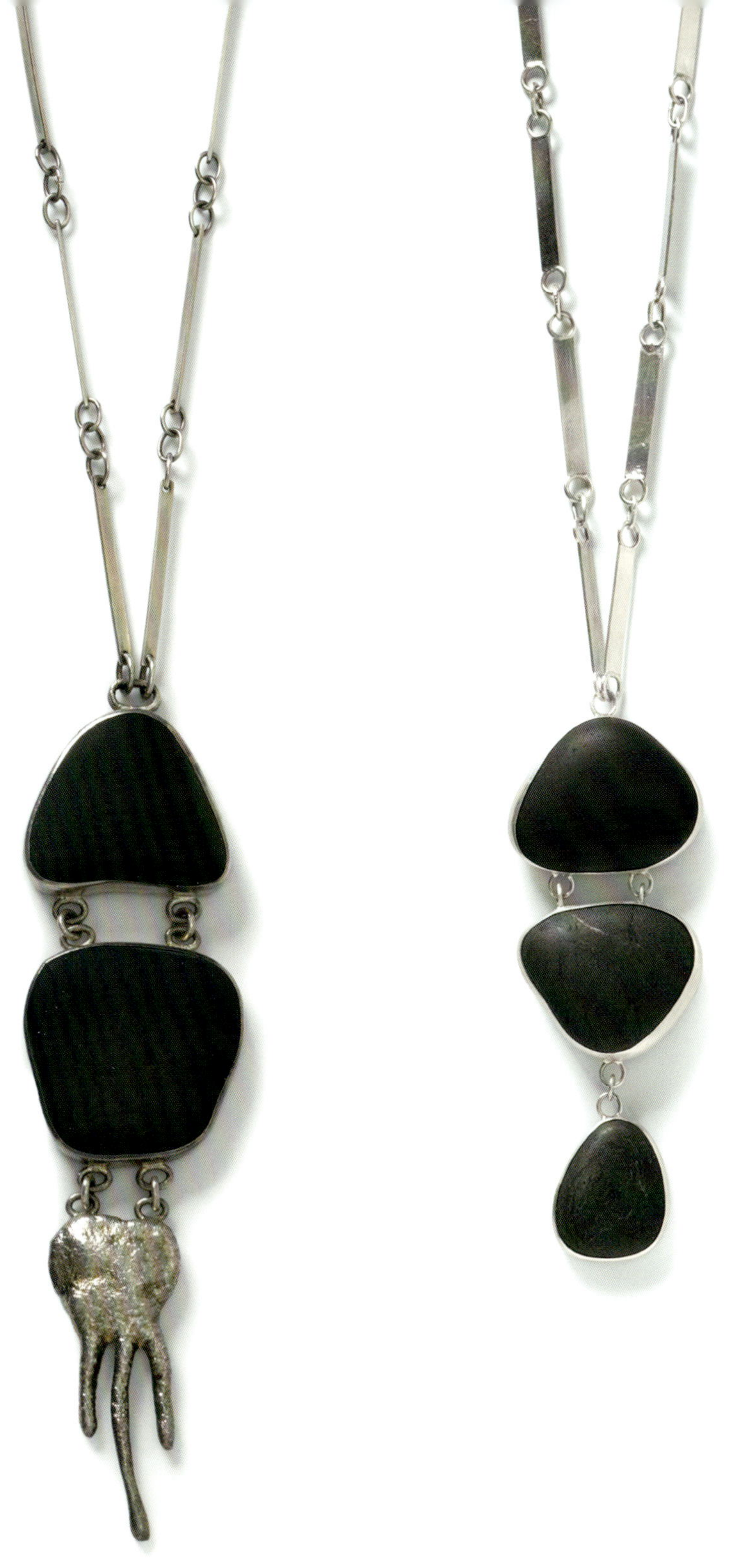

Anhänger | pendant, 1965
Silber, Kieselsteine | silver, pebble stones
H. 14,8 cm, B. 3,9 cm | h. 14,8 cm, w. 3,9 cm
Privatbesitz | private property

Anhänger | pendant, 1961
Silber, Kieselsteine | silver, pebble stones
H. 9,5 cm, B. 3,7 cm | h. 9,5 cm, w. 3,7 cm
Privatbesitz | private property

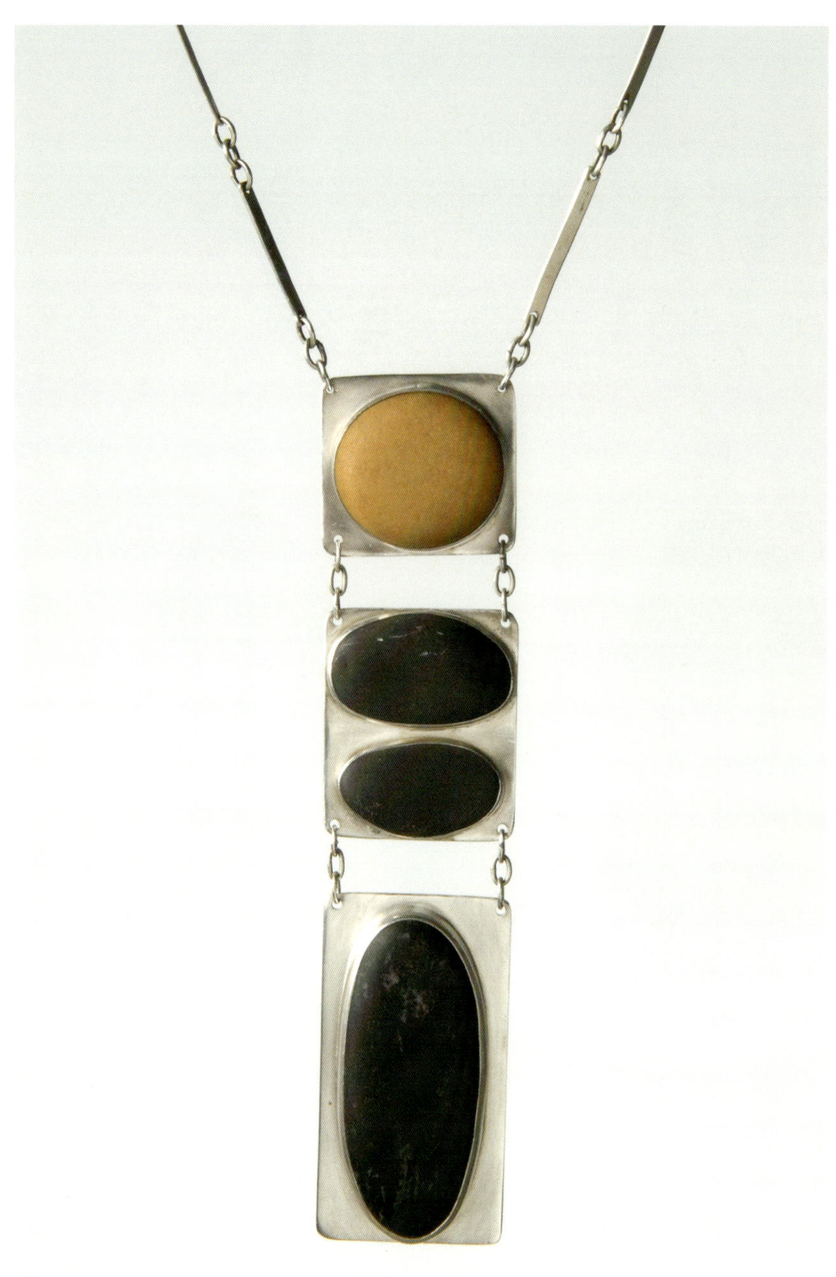

Halsschmuck | necklace, 1961
Silber, Kieselsteine | silver, pebble stones
L. 44 cm, B. 3,5 cm | l. 44 cm, w. 3,5 cm
Die Neue Sammlung – The Design Museum
Dauerleihgabe der Danner-Stiftung München
permanent loan of the Danner Foundation Munich

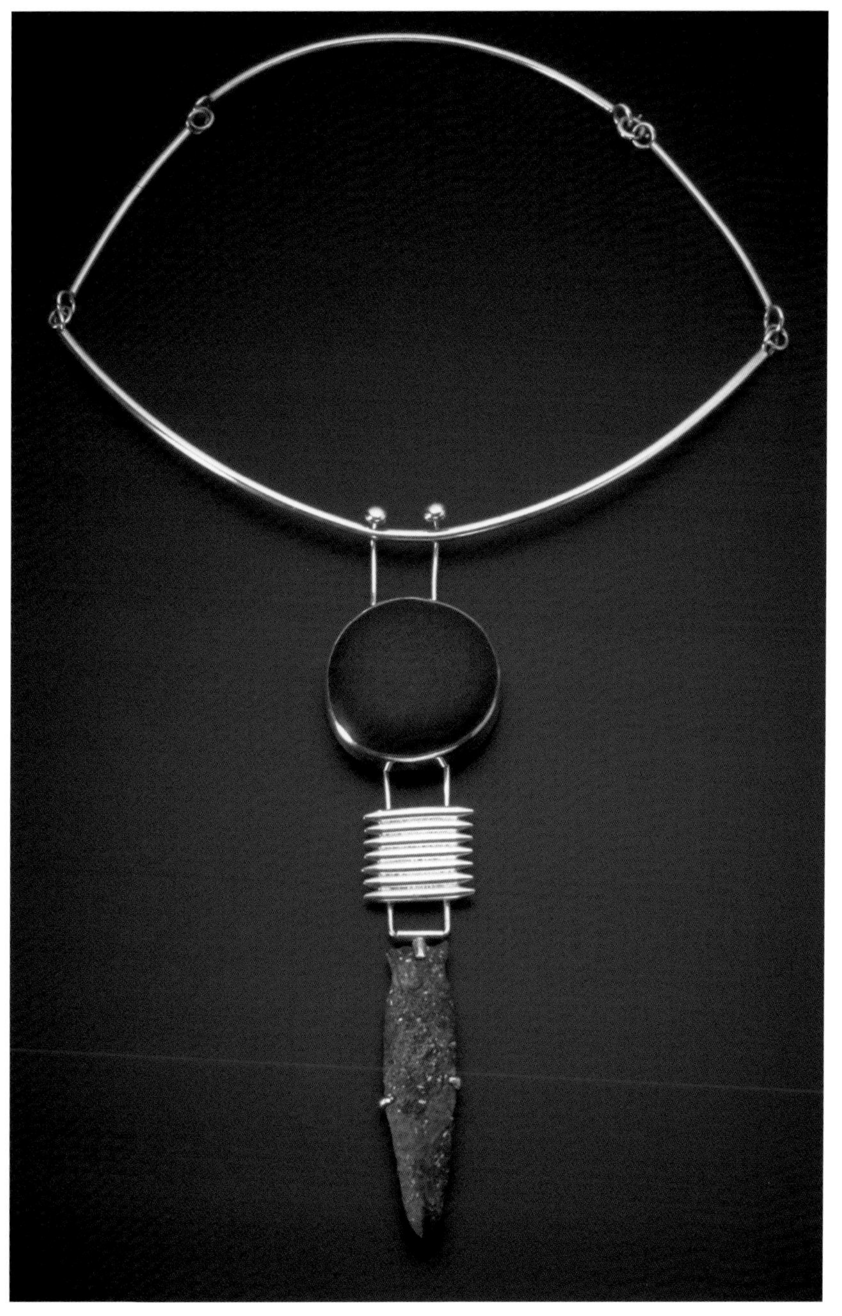

Halsschmuck | necklace, 1966
Silber, Pfeilspitze | silver, arrowhead (Red Indian Stone)
H. 17 cm, B. 19 cm | h. 17 cm, w 19 cm
Collection: The Worshipful Company of Goldsmiths

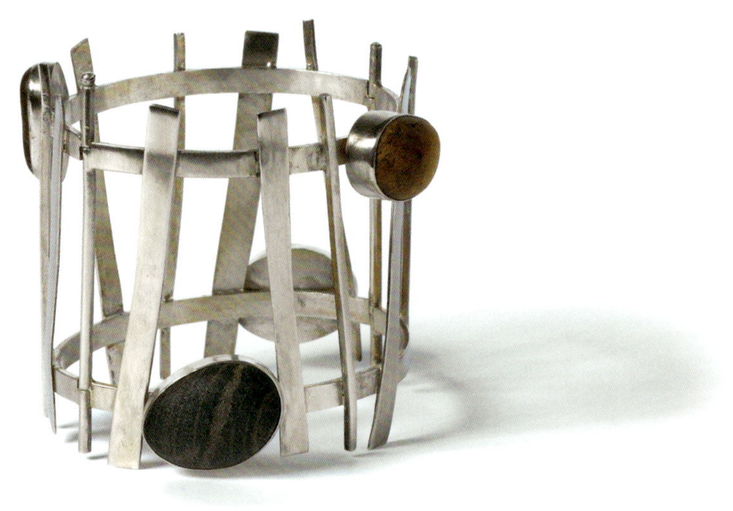

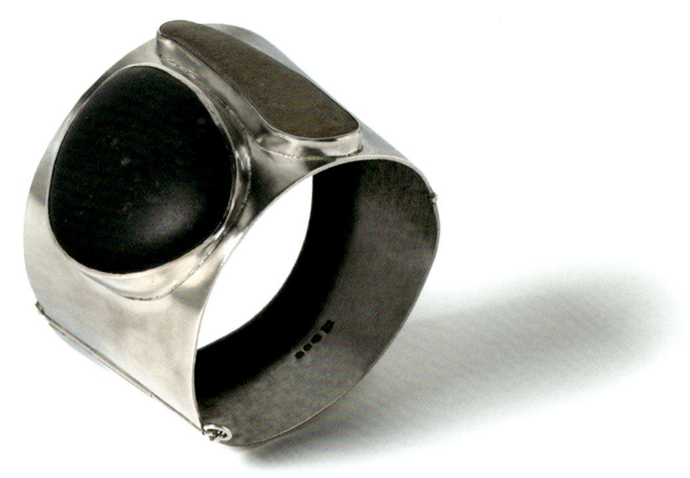

Armschmuck | bracelet, 1960
Silber, Kieselsteine | silver, pebble stones
H. 7 cm, B. 8 cm, T. 7,5 cm
h. 7 cm, w. 8 cm, d. 7,5 cm
Die Neue Sammlung – The Design Museum
Dauerleihgabe der Danner-Stiftung München
permanent loan of the Danner Foundation Munich

Armschmuck | bracelet, 1960
Silber, Kieselsteine | silver, pebble stones
H. 5,5 cm, B. 6,8 cm | h. 5,5 cm, w. 6,8 cm
Privatbesitz | private property

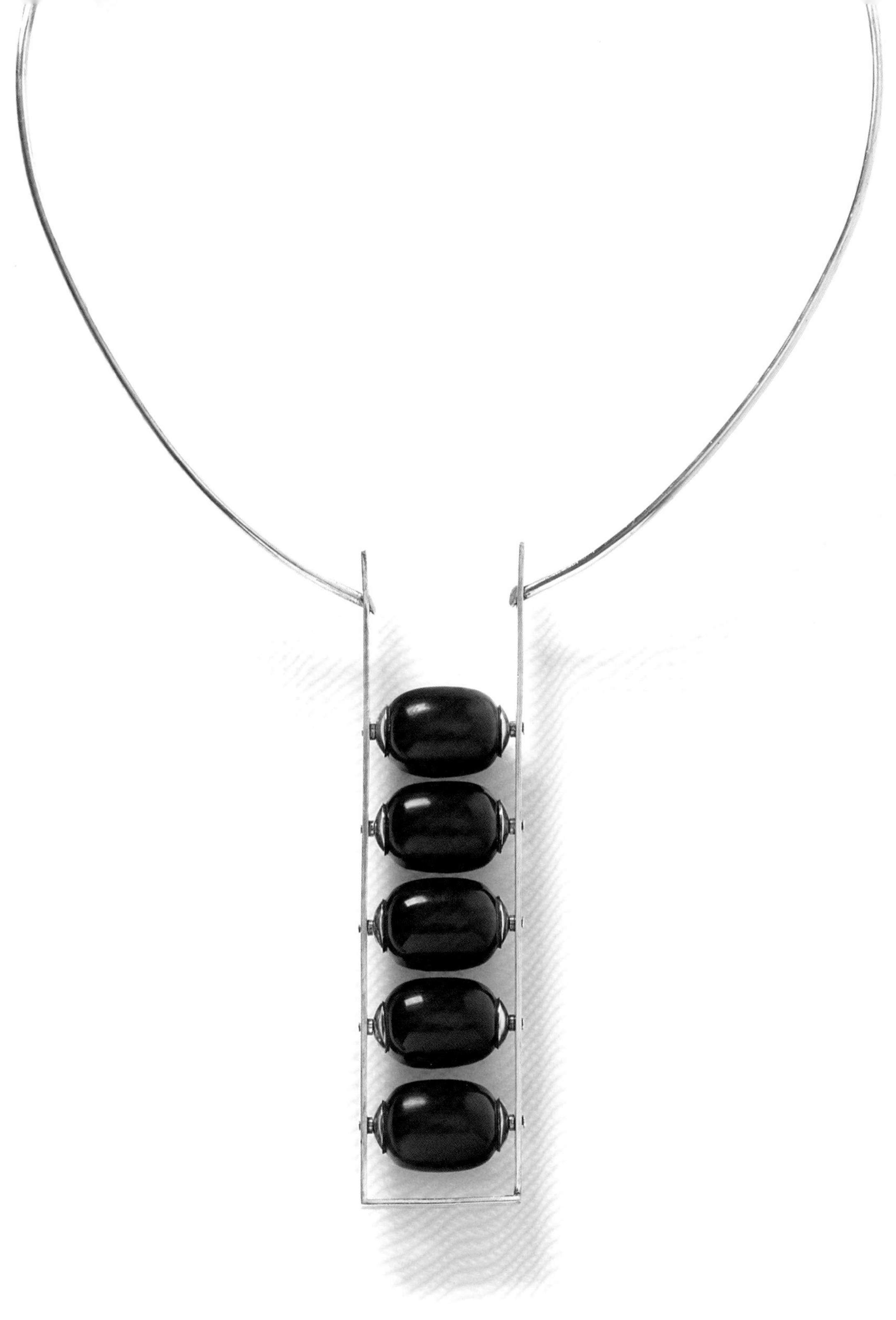

Anhänger | pendant, 1969
Silber, Bernstein | silver, amber
H. 15,3 cm, B. 4 cm, T. 1,7 cm
h. 15,3 cm, w. 4 cm, d. 1,7 cm
Privatbesitz | private property

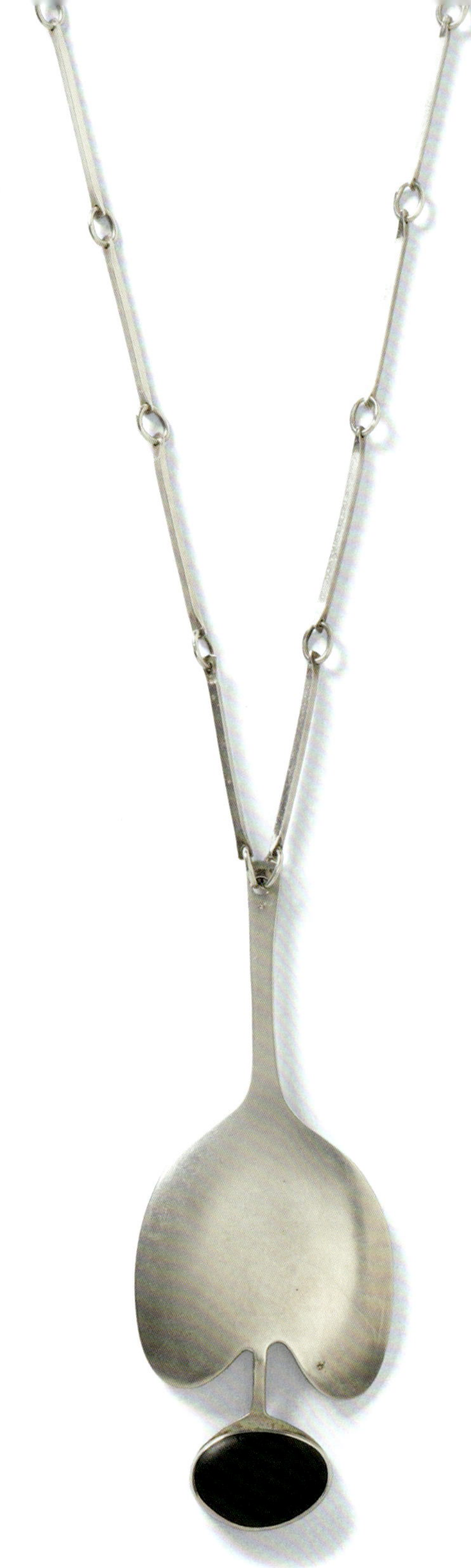

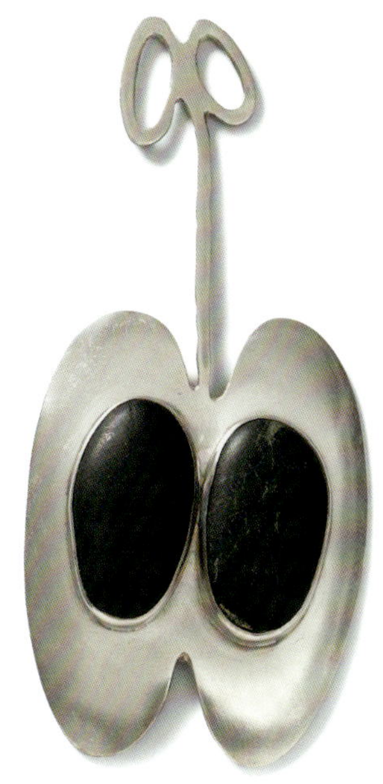

Halsschmuck, 1964 oder 1966 | necklace 1964 or 1966
Silber, Kieselstein | silver, pebble stone
H. 10,6 cm, B. 4,2 cm | h. 10,6 cm, w. 4,2 cm
Privatbesitz | private property

Anhänger | pendant, 1971
Silber, Kieselsteine | silver, pebble stones
H. 11,8 cm, B. 5,7 cm | h. 11,8 cm, w. 5,7 cm
Privatbesitz | private property

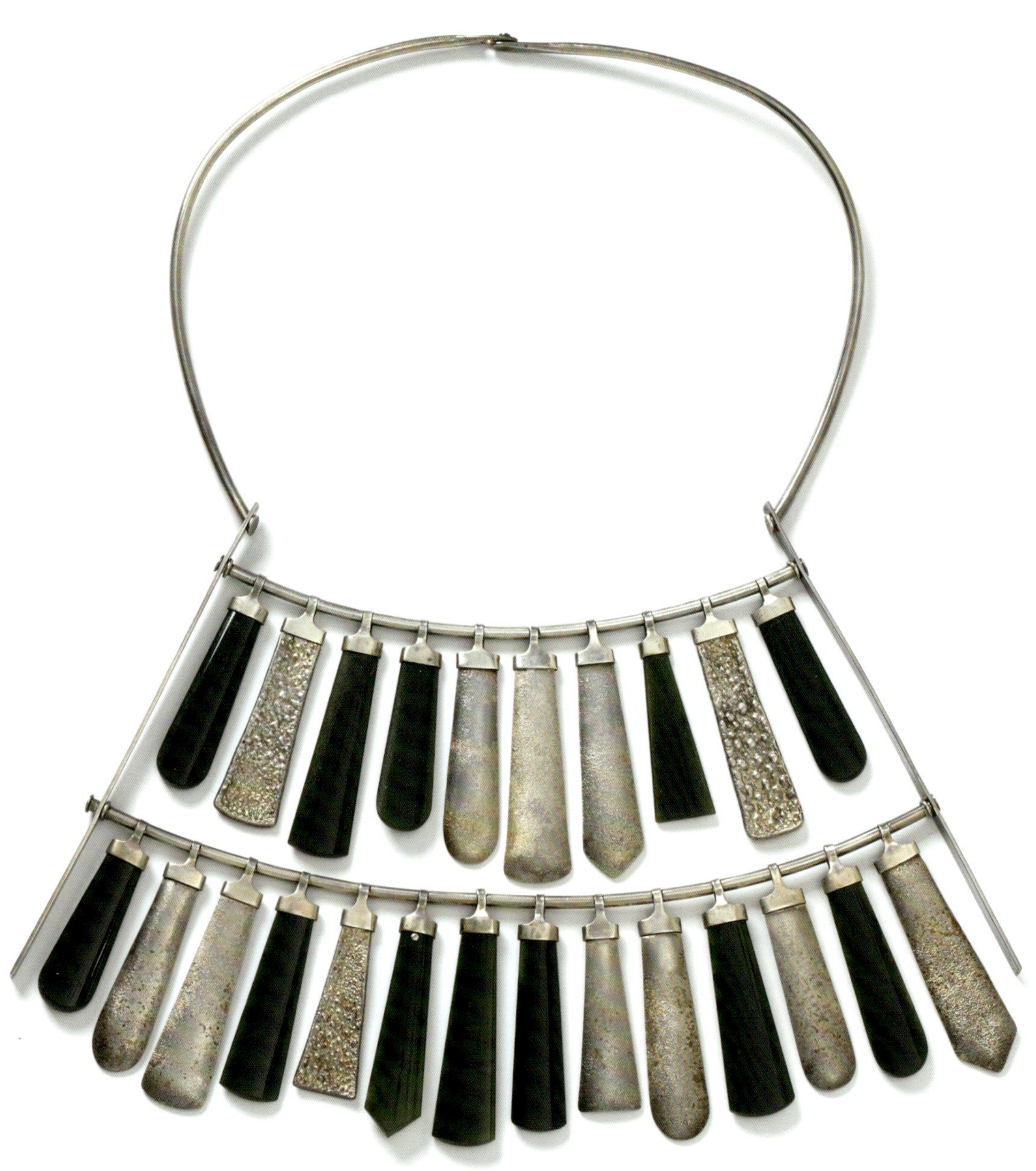

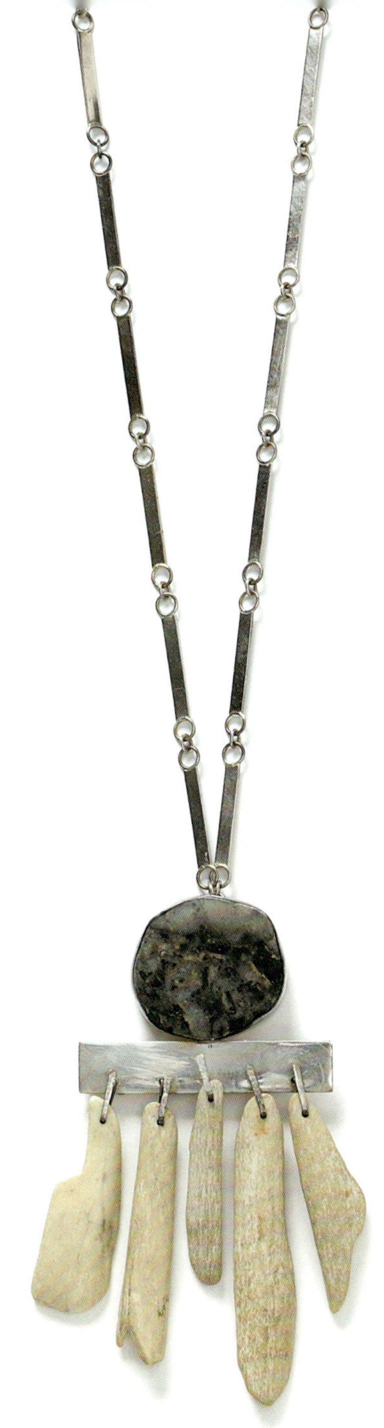

Halsschmuck | necklace, 1967
Silber, Achate | silver, agates
H. 19 cm, B. 17,2 cm | h. 19 cm, w. 17,2 cm
Privatbesitz | private property

Anhänger | pendant, 1968
Silber, Terrazzo, Knochen | silver, terrazzo, bones
H. 12 cm, B. 6,3 cm | h. 12 cm, w. 6,3 cm
Privatbesitz | private property

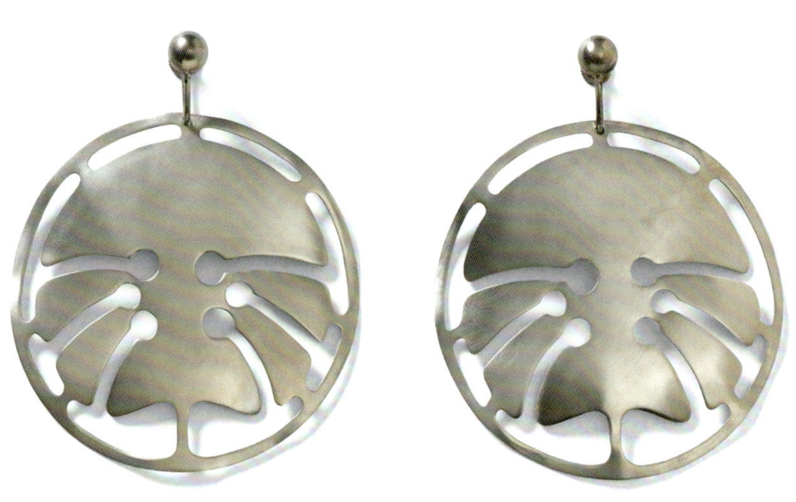

Ohrschmuck | earrings, 1967
Silber | silver
H. 5,9 cm, B. 6 cm | h. 5,9 cm, w. 6 cm
Privatbesitz | private property

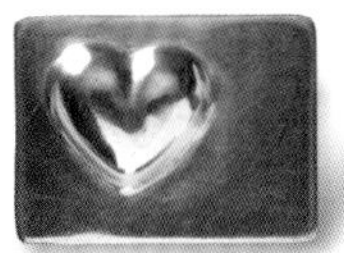
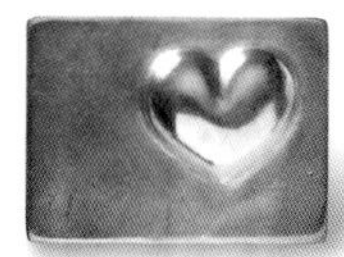
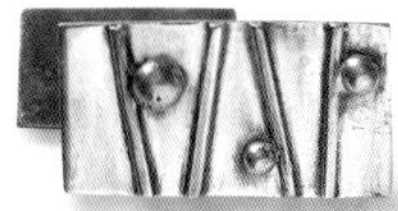
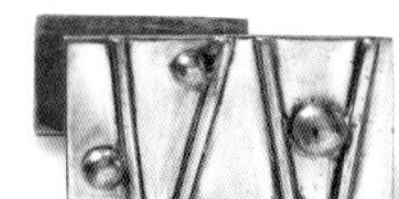
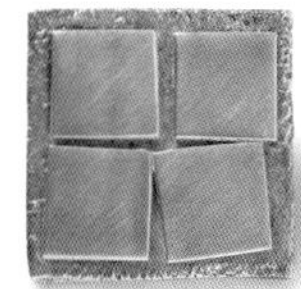
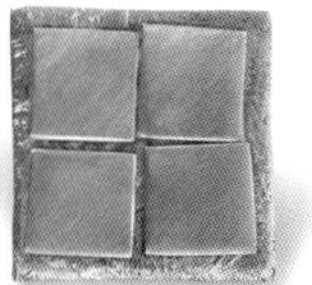
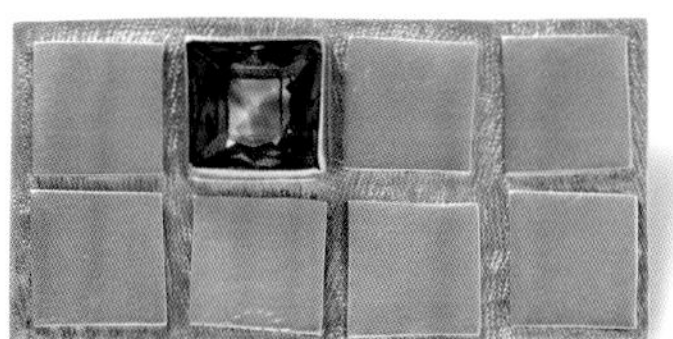

Manschettenknöpfe | cufflinks, 1961
Silber | silver
H. 1,3–1,8 cm, B. 2,5–2,6 cm | h. 1,3–1,8 cm, w. 2,5–2,6 cm
Privatbesitz | private property

Brosche und Manschettenknöpfe | brooch and cufflinks, 1967
Silber, Amethyst | silver, amethyst
Brosche: H. 2,4 cm, L. 5 cm | brooch: h. 2,4 cm, l. 5 cm
Manschettenknöpfe: H. 2,1 cm, B. 2,2 cm | cufflinks: h. 2,1 cm, w. 2,2 cm
Privatbesitz | private property

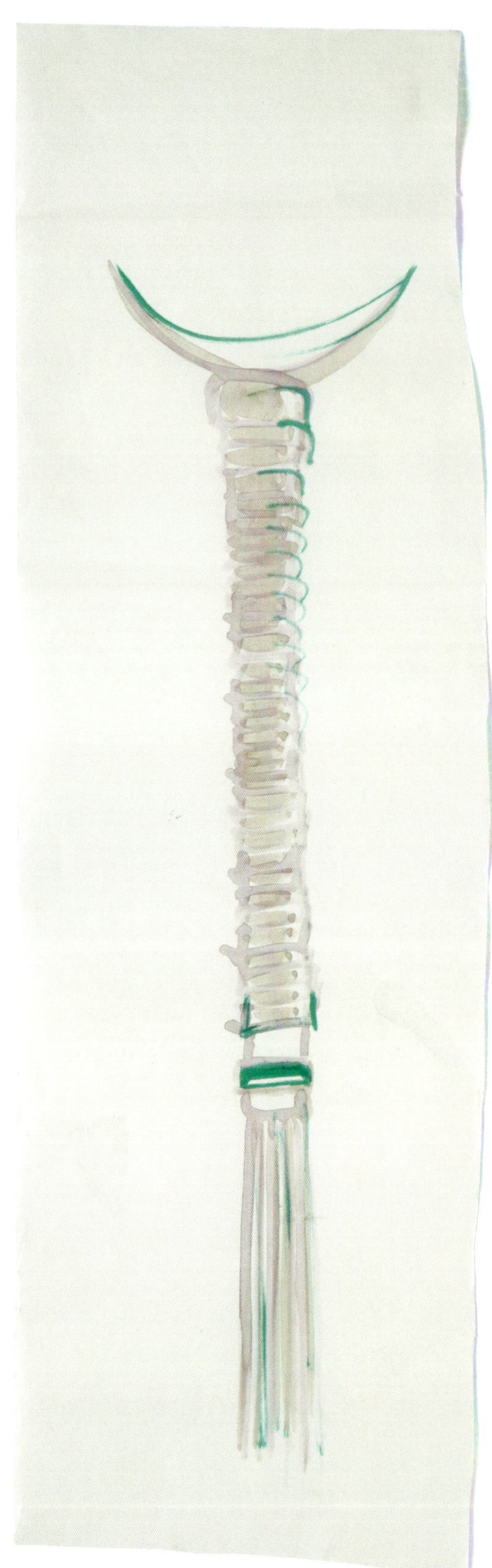

Entwurfszeichnung für einen Halsschmuck
scetch for a necklace, 1968–1971(?)
Papier, Filzstift, Aquarellfarbe
paper, felt pen, watercolour
H. 61 cm, B. 19,8 cm | h. 61 cm, w. 19,8 cm
Die Neue Sammlung – The Design Museum

Halsschmuck | necklace, 1968–1971 (?)
Gold, Amethyst | gold, amethyst
H. 46 cm, B. 2–12,5 cm | h. 46 cm, w. 2–12,5 cm
Privatbesitz | private property

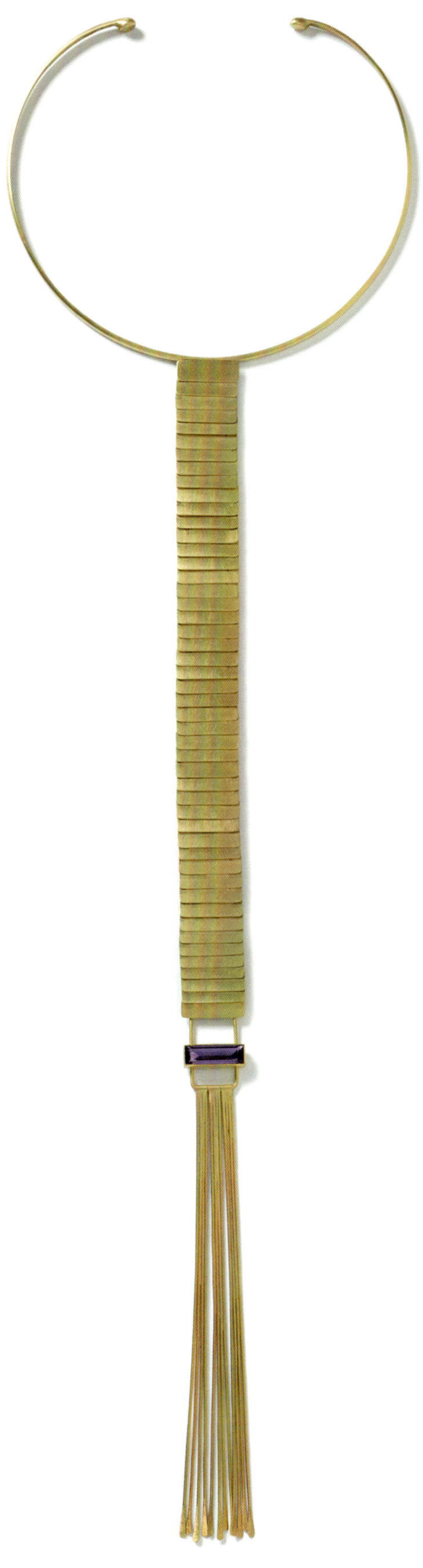

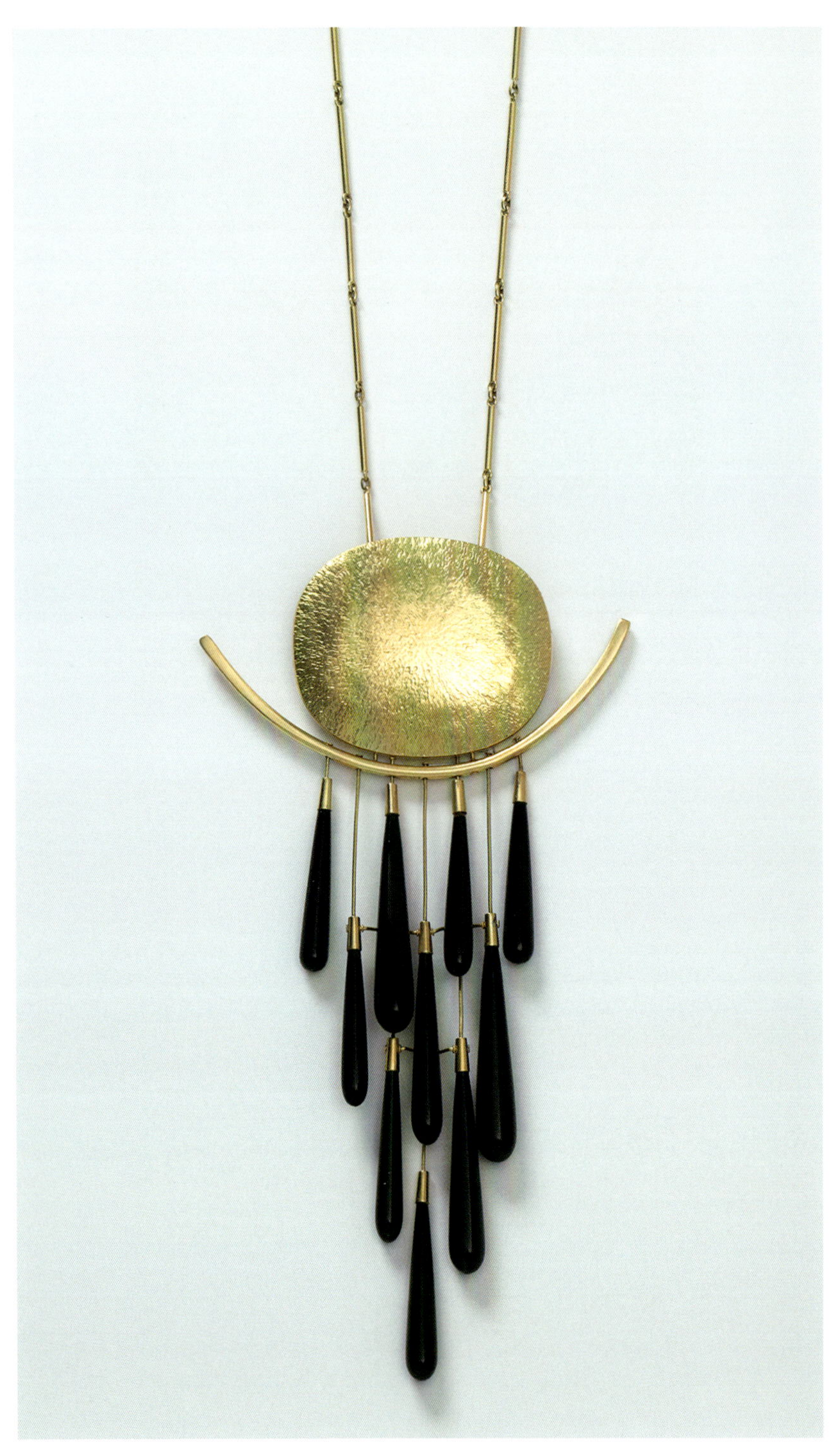

Halsschmuck | necklace, 1968
Gold, Achate | gold, agates
H. 42 cm, B. 10,4 cm | h. 42 cm, w. 10,4 cm
Privatbesitz | private property

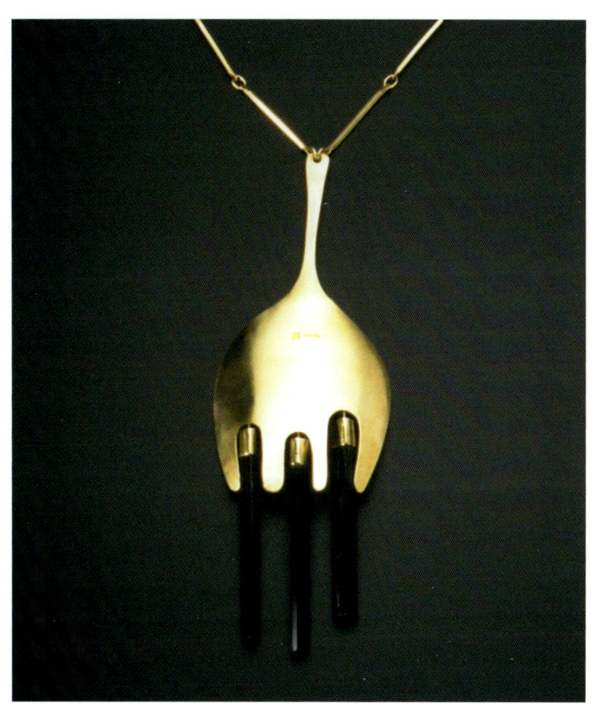

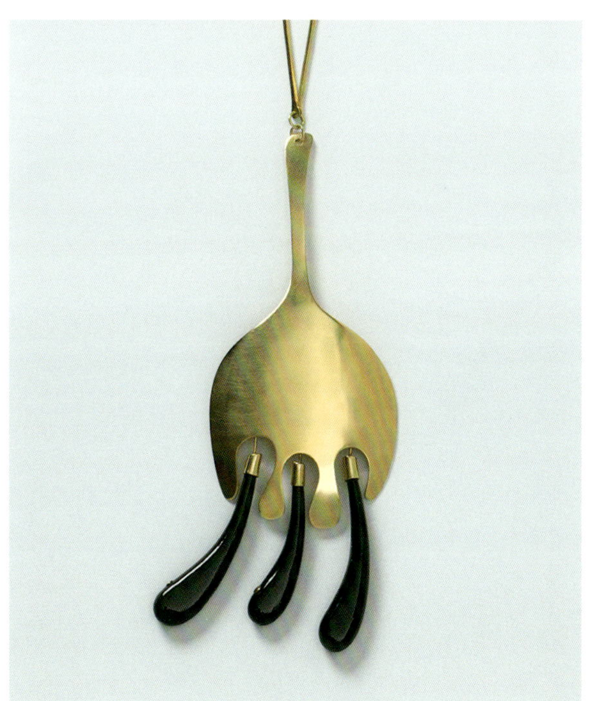

Anhänger | pendant, 1966
Gold, Turmaline | gold, turmalines
H. 14 cm, B. 4,7 cm
h. 14 cm, w. 4,7 cm
Collection: The Worshipful Company of Goldsmiths

Anhänger | pendant, 1966
Greengold, Jade
greengold, jade
H. 12,7 cm, B. 4,8 cm
h. 12,7 cm, w. 4,8 cm
Privatbesitz | private property

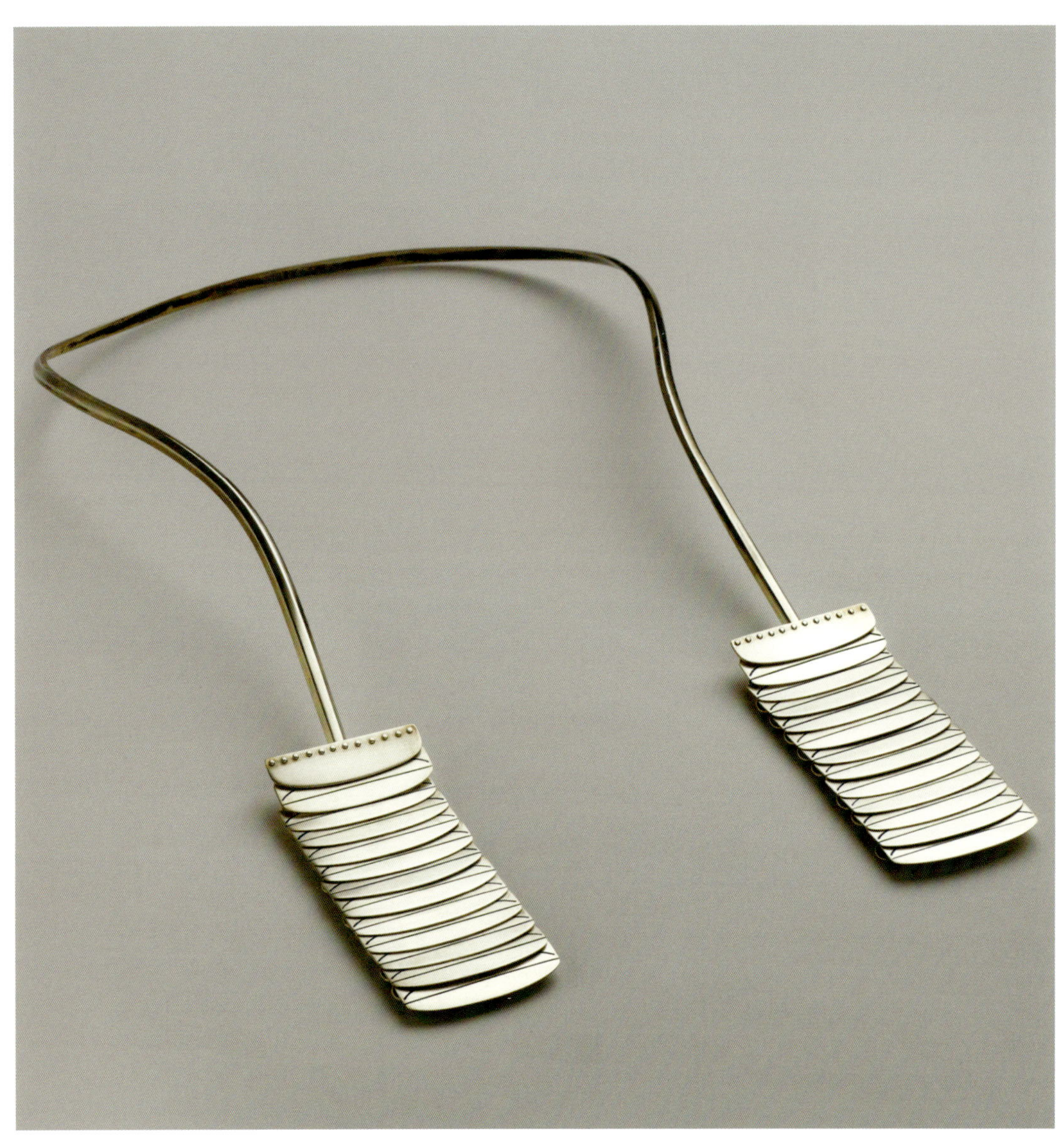

Halsschmuck | necklace, 1976
Silber, Emaille | silver, enamel
H. 29 cm | h. 29 cm
Crafts Council, London–
Foto: John Donat

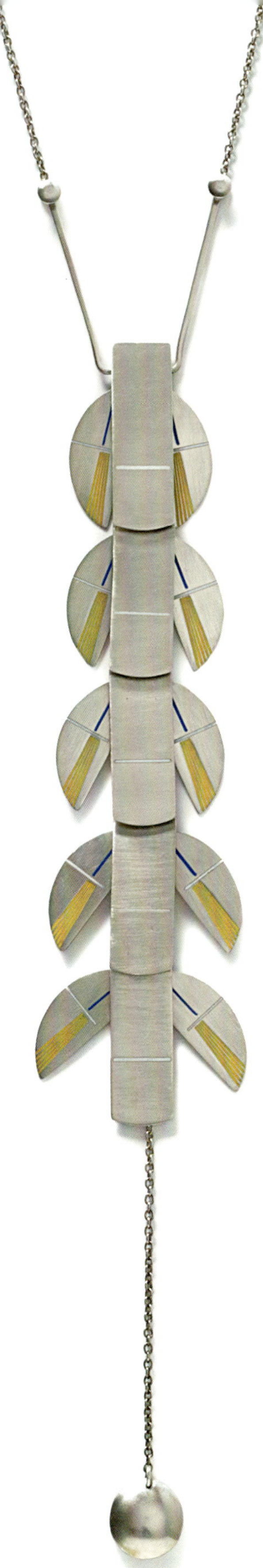

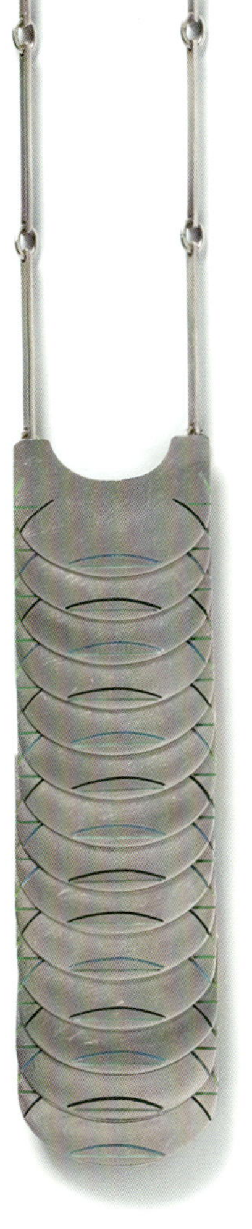

Halsschmuck – kinetisch | necklace – kinetic, 1971
Silber, Emaille | silver, enamel
H. 50 cm, B. 3–5 cm | h. 50 cm, w. 3–5 cm
Die Neue Sammlung – The Design Museum.
Dauerleihgabe der Danner-Stiftung München
permanent loan of the Danner Foundation Munich

Anhänger | pendant, 1968/1971
Silber, Emaille | silver, enamel
H. 11,5 cm, B. 3,3 cm | h. 11,5 cm, w. 3,3 cm
Privatbesitz | private property

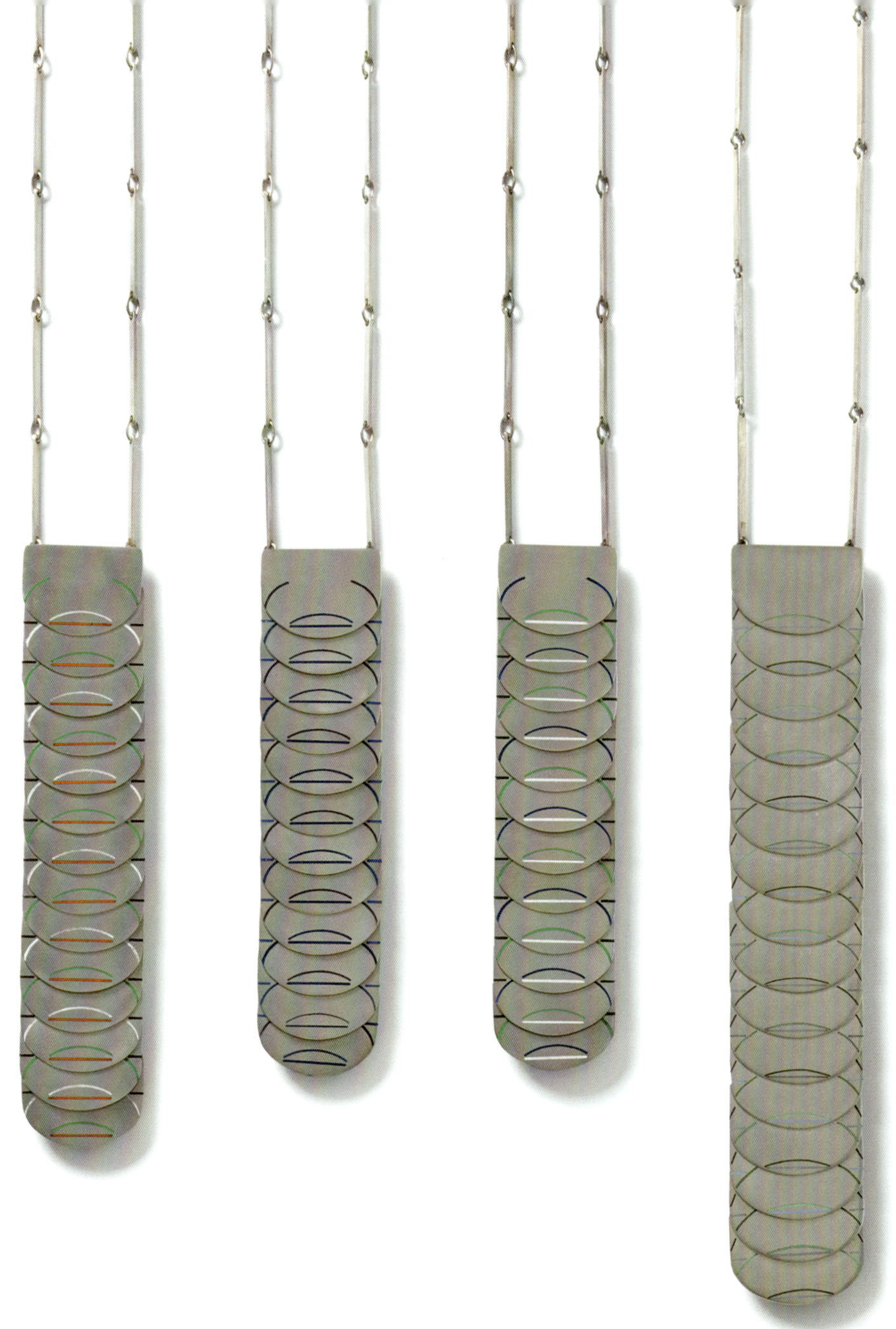

Anhänger | pendants, 1968/1971
Silber, Emaille | silver, enamel
H. 12,8–18 cm, B. 3–3,3 cm | h. 12,8–18 cm, w. 3–3,3 cm
Privatbesitz | private property

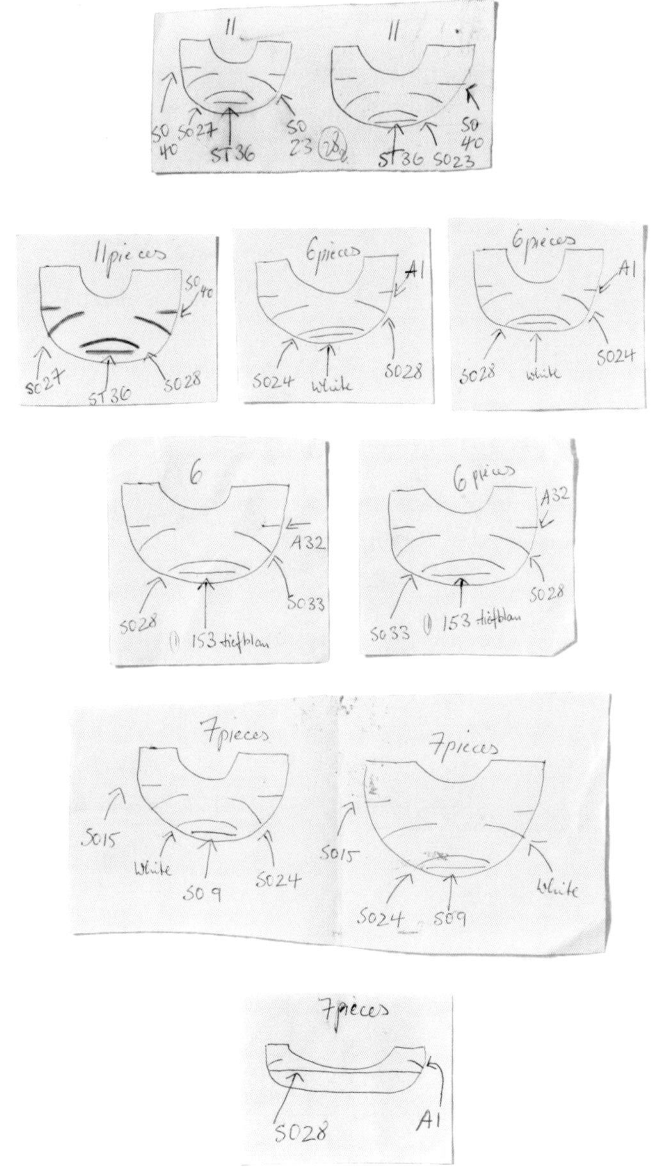

Entwurfszeichnungen mit Farbangaben für einen Anhänger
scetches with colour informations for a pendant, 1968/1971
Papier, Kugelschreiber, Filzstift | paper, ballpoint pen, felt pen
H. 4,3–7,9 cm, B. 6,1–16,7 cm | h. 4,3–7,9 cm, w. 6,1–16,7 cm
Die Neue Sammlung – The Design Museum

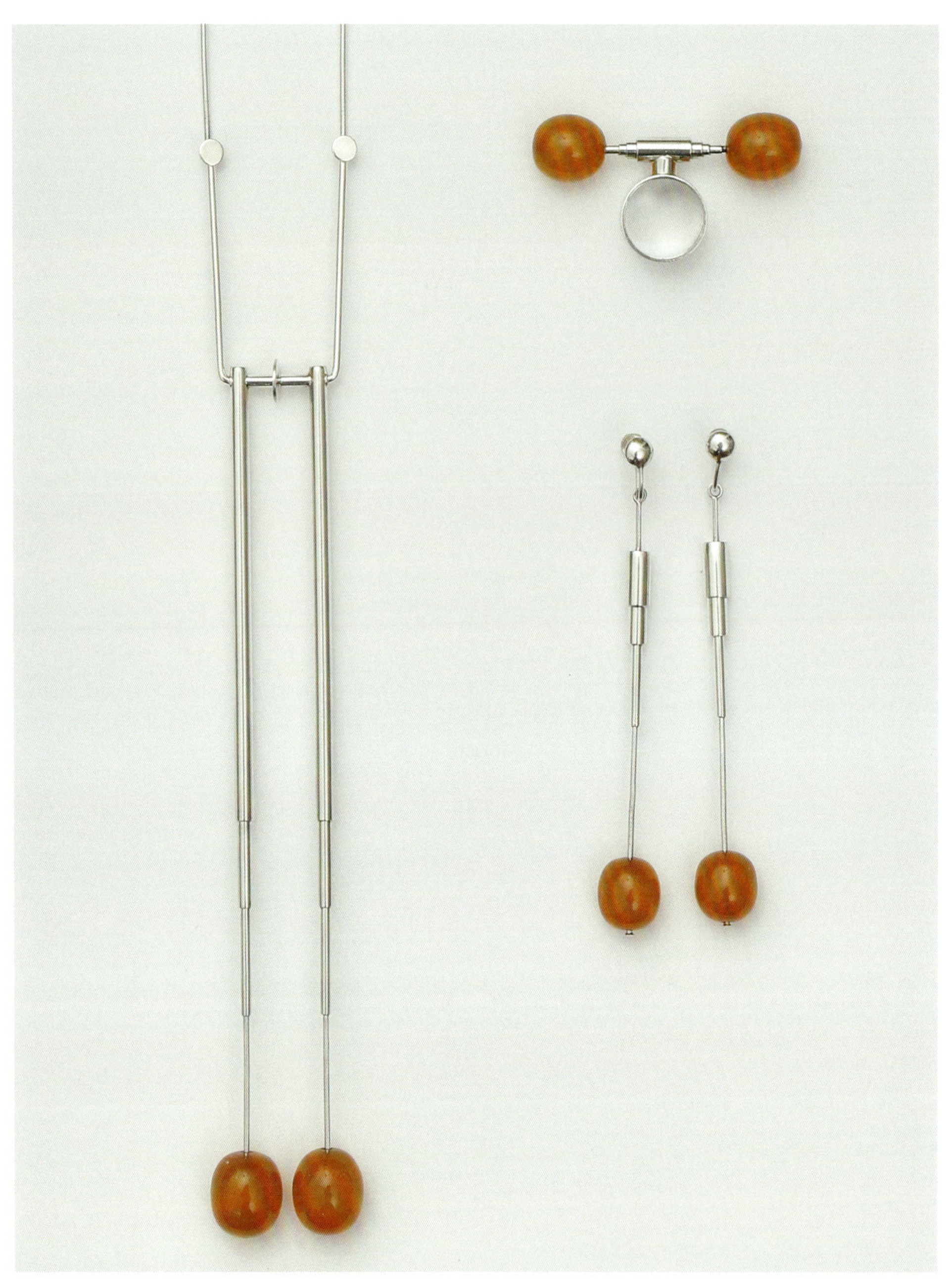

Garnitur | set, 1968
Silber, Bernstein | silver, amber
Anhänger: H. 19 cm | pendant: h. 19 cm
Ring: H. 6 cm| ring: h. 6 cm
Ohrschmuck: H. 8,5 cm | earrings: h. 8,5 cm
Museum Angewandte Kunst Frankfurt
Foto: Uwe Dettmar Gerader

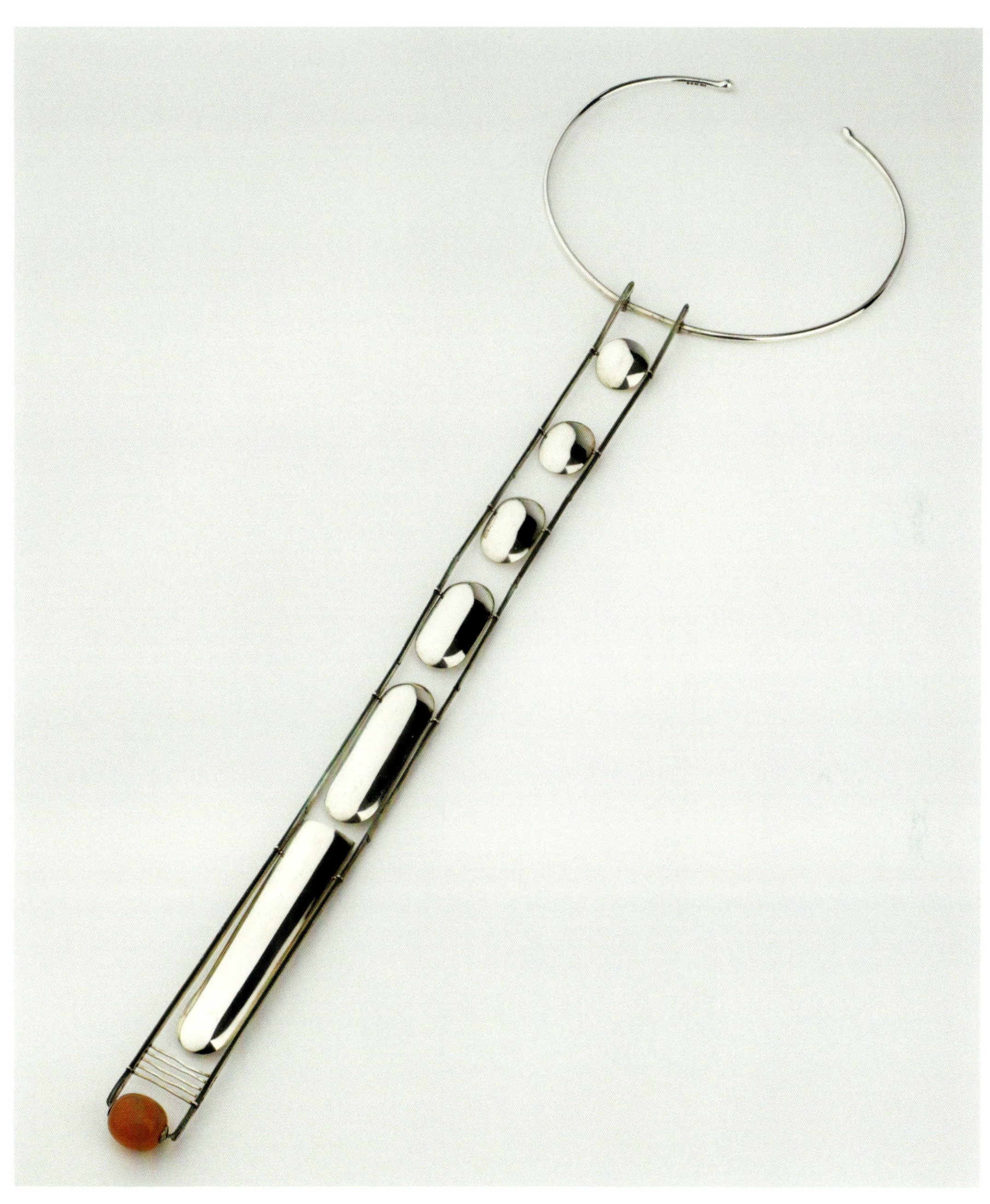

Foto: David Cripps, 1976
Halsschmuck von Helga Zahn | necklace by Helga Zahn, 1972–1974
Silber, Kunststoff, Bernstein | silver, plastics, amber
H. 38 cm, Dm. 15 cm | h. 38 cm, diam. 15 cm
Crafts Council, London

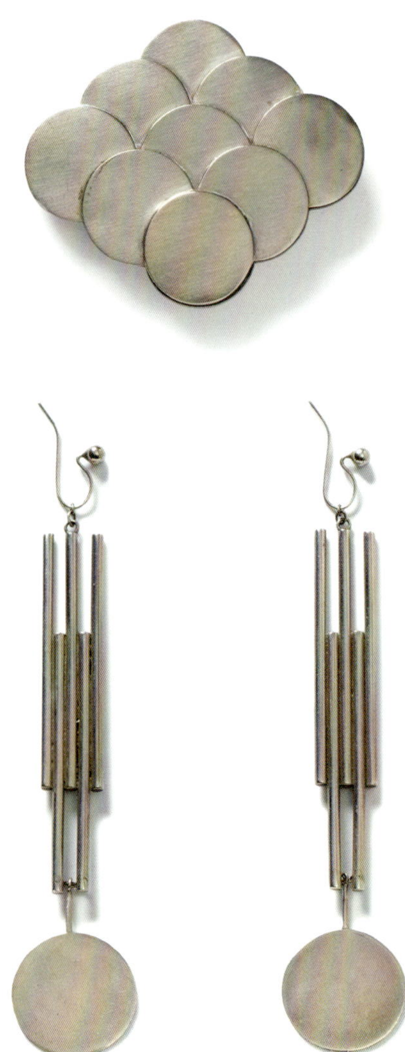

Brosche | brooch, 1970 (?)
Silber | silver
H. 4 cm, B. 4,8 cm
h. 4 cm, w. 4,8 cm
Privatbesitz | private property

Ohrschmuck | earrings, 1967/1968
Silber | silver
H. 8,2 cm, B. 2,1 cm
h. 8,2 cm, w. 2,1 cm
Privatbesitz | private property

Halsschmuck | necklace, 1967
Silber, Onyx | silver, onyx
H. 27 cm, B. 24,2 cm
h. 27 cm, w. 24,2 cm
Privatbesitz | private property

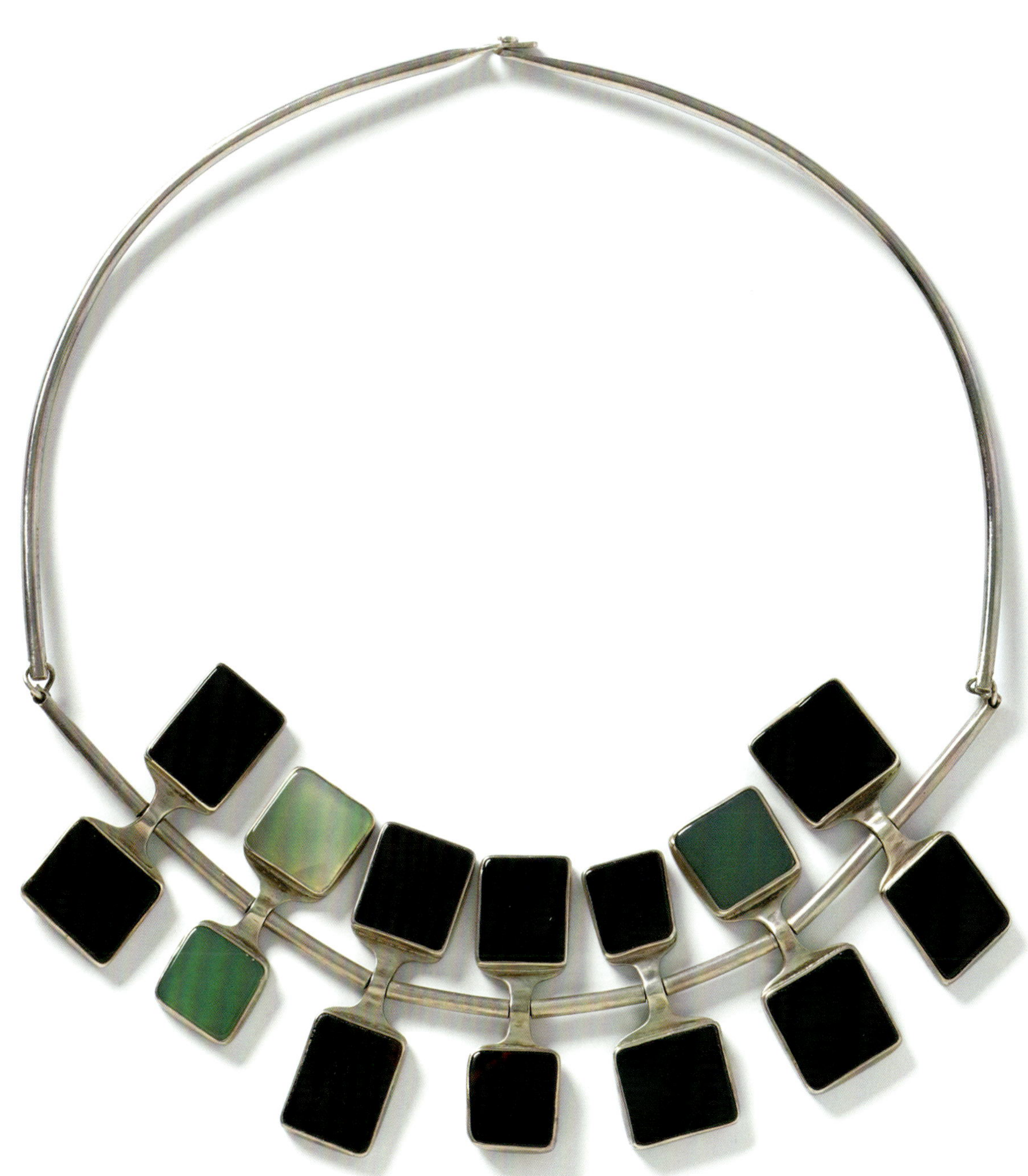

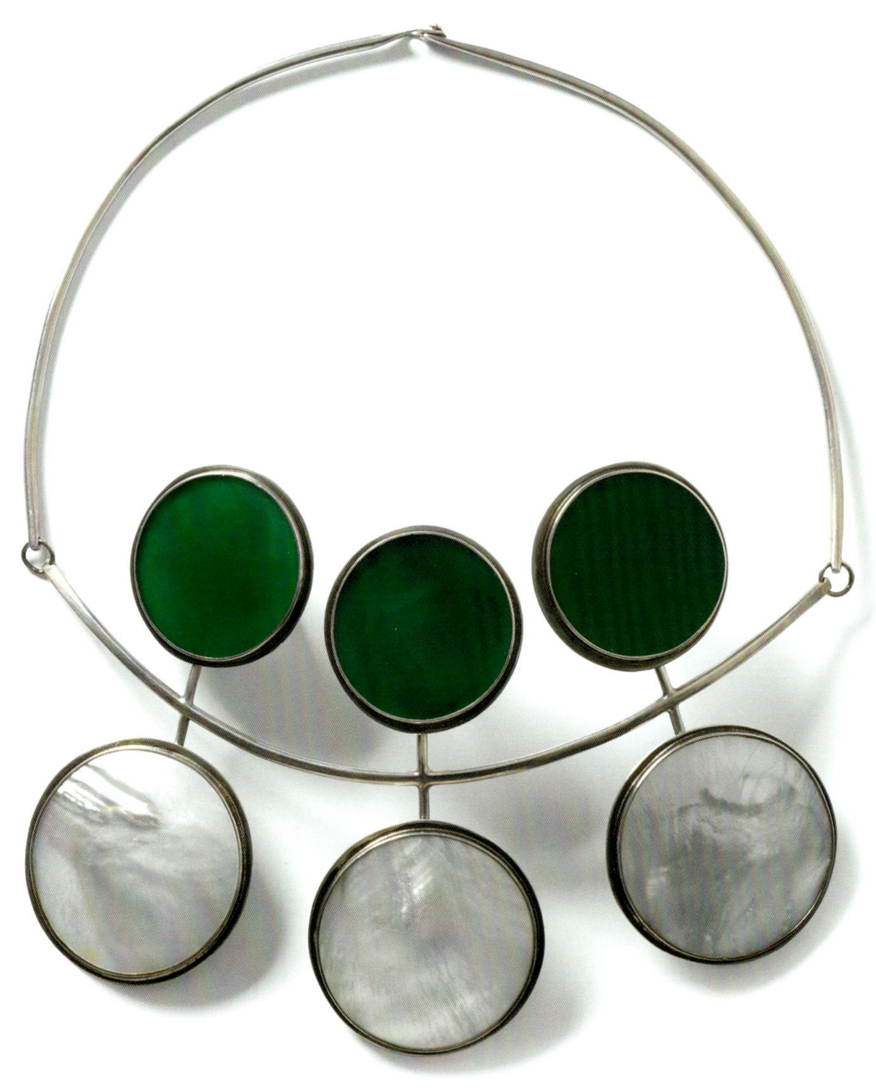

Halsschmuck | necklace, 1966
Silber, Achate, Perlmutt | silver, agates, mother-of-pearl
H. 22,8 cm, B. 19 cm | h. 22,8 cm, w. 19 cm
Privatbesitz | private property

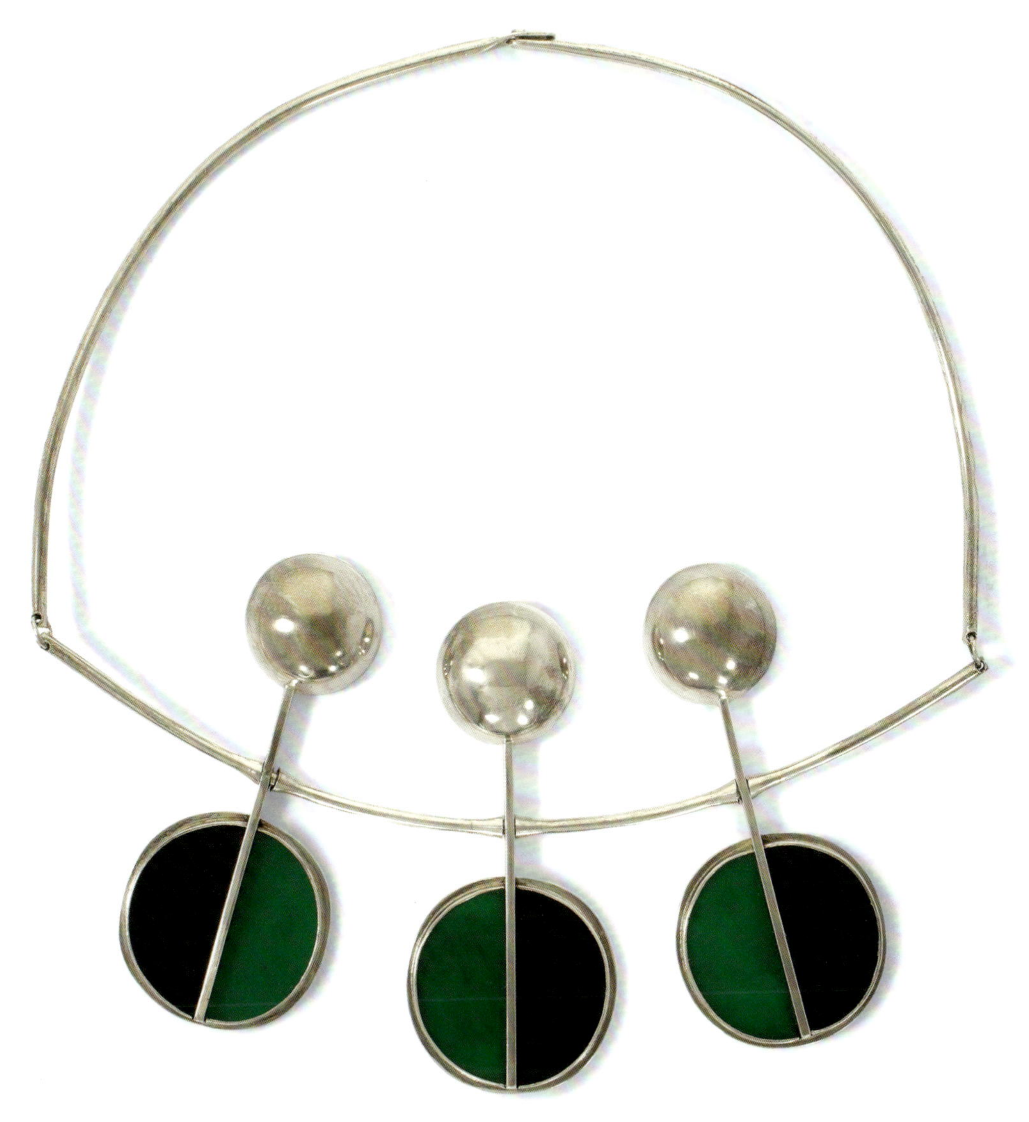

Halsschmuck | necklace, 1966
Silber, Onyx, Quarz | silver, onyx, quartz
H. 20,5 cm, B. 19 cm | h. 20,5 cm, w. 19 cm
Staatliche Museen zu Berlin – Kunstgewerbemuseum
Foto: Karen Bartsch

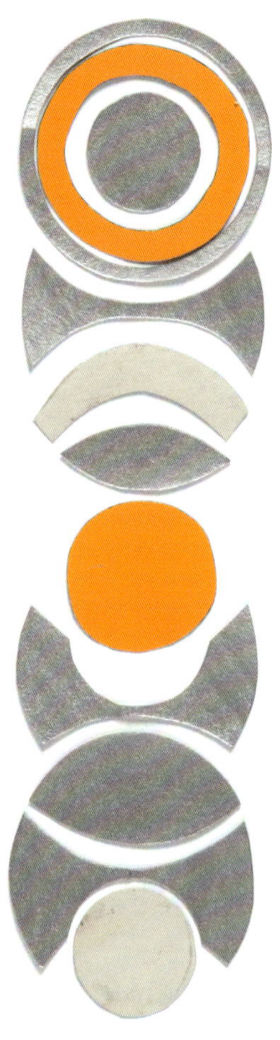

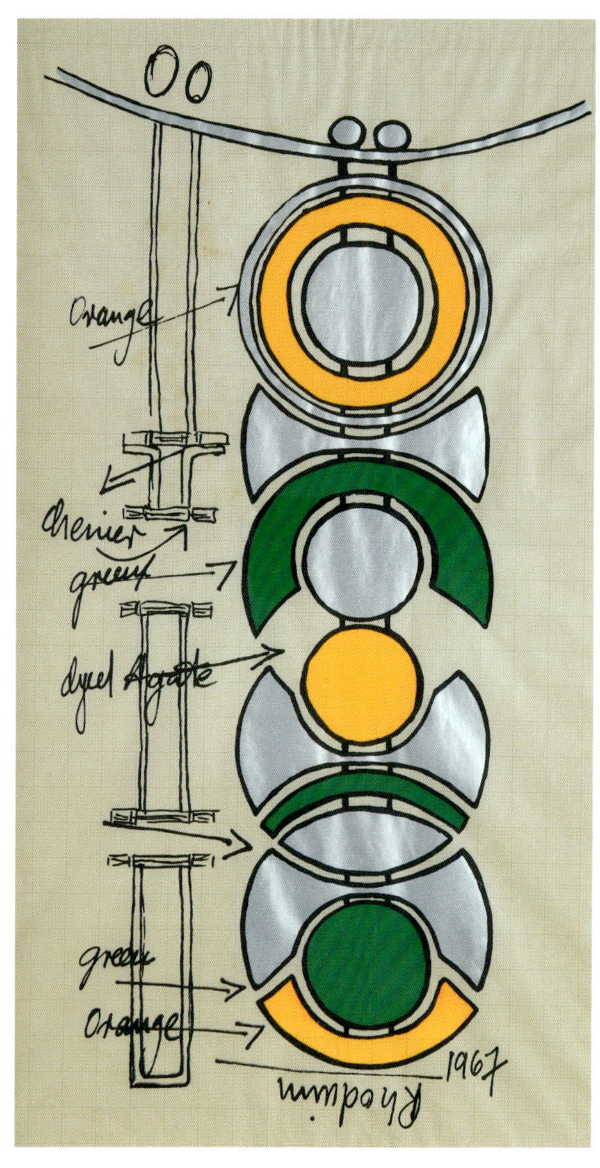

Schnittschablonen für einen Halsschmuck
cutting stencils for a necklace, 1967
Karton, Bleistift | cardboard, pencil
Die Neue Sammlung – The Design Museum

Entwurf für einen Halsschmuck | scetch for a necklace, 1967
Papier, Tusche, Farbe | paper, ink, paint
H. 85 cm, B. 55 cm | h. 85 cm, w. 55 cm
Privatbesitz | private property

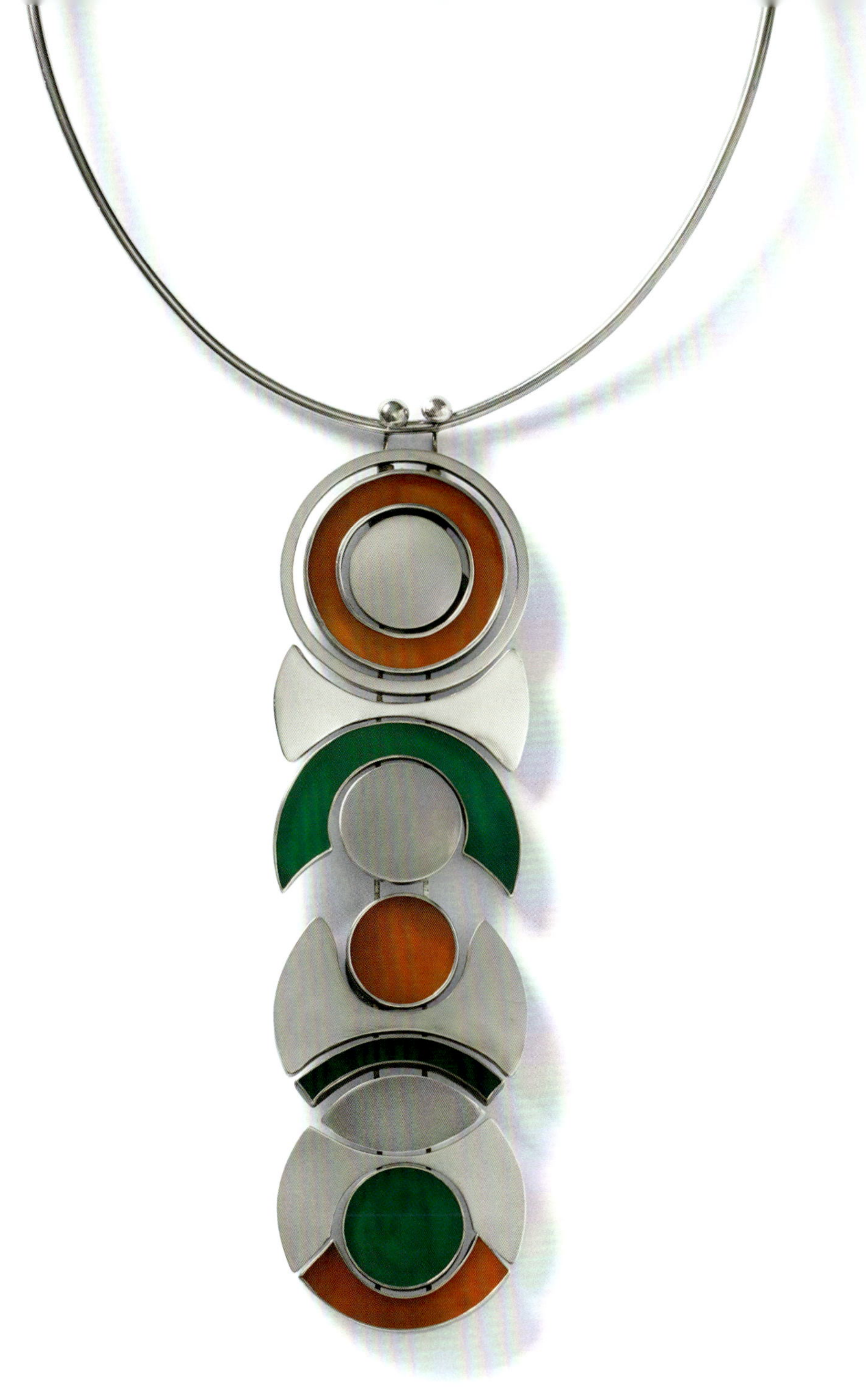

Halsschmuck | necklace, 1967
Silber, Achate | silver, agates
H. 20,4 cm, B. 5,6 cm | h. 20,4 cm, w. 5.6 cm
Privatbesitz | private property

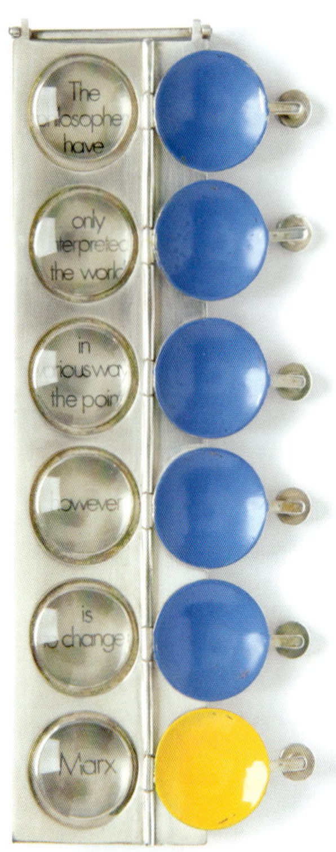

Brosche „Cartier's Revolutionary Display Tray" | brooch "Cartier's Revolutionary Display Tray", 1968
Silber, Emaille, optisches Glas | silver, enamel, optical glass
H. 13,5 cm, B. 3,4–5 cm | h. 13,5 cm, w. 3,4–5 cm
Die Neue Sammlung – The Design Museum.
Dauerleihgabe der Danner-Stiftung München | permanent loan of the Danner Foundation Munich

… die „coole Tante Helga" mit rötlichem gefärbtem glattem Haar und den langen dunkelroten oder dunkel-lila Schlabber-Samtkleidern

Tine Waldenfels, Nichte [32]

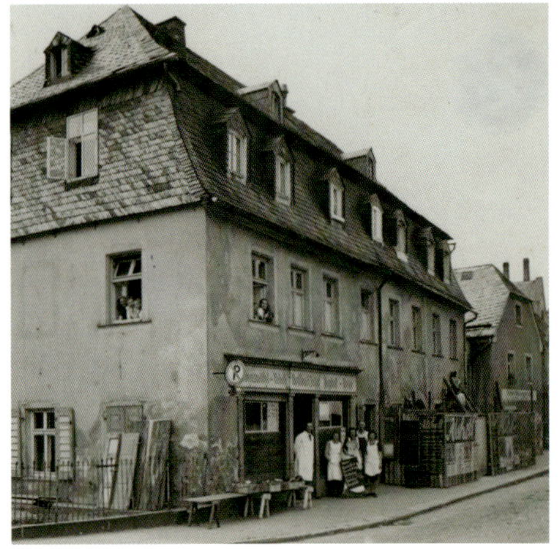

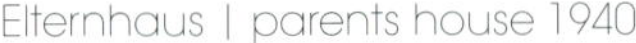

Elternhaus | parents house 1940

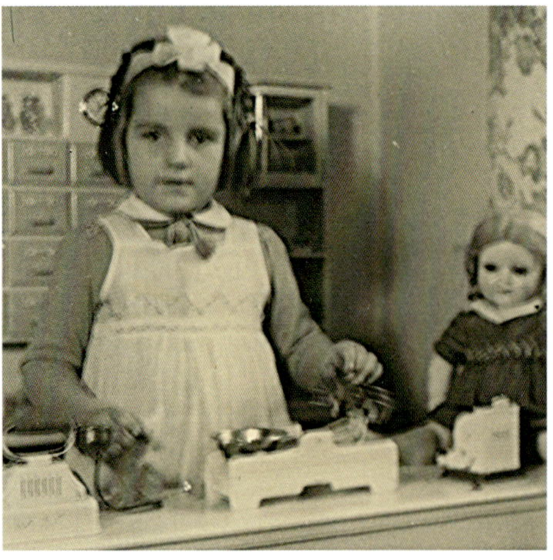

Als Dreijährige | in the age of three

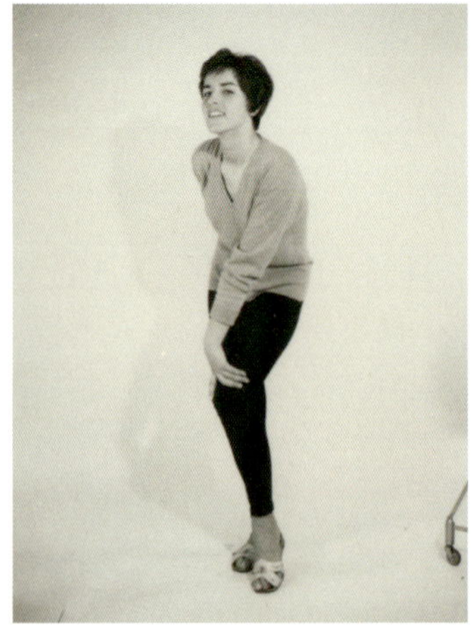

Als Model | as a model 1958

Biografie | biography

13.11.1936
geboren in Hof und aufgewachsen in Schwarzenbach an der Saale | born in Hof and raised in Schwarzenbach an der Saale

1943–1951
Volksschule, Realschule | elementary and secondary school

1954
Abschluss kaufmännische Berufsschule | graduation professional school
Tätig im elterlichen Lebensmittelgeschäft in Schwarzenbach | working in the grocery store of her parents in Schwarzenbach

1955
Assistenz in Fotoabteilung eines Drogeriegeschäfts in Kronach | assisting in the photo department of a drugstore in Kronach

1956
London, Großbritannien | Great Britain
Arbeitet als Haushaltshilfe | working as domestic help

1957
Sprachzertifikat | Language Certificate "Lower Cambridge Certificate Elementary"

1958
Kennenlernen des Grafikers und Designers Peter Gee | meets the printmaker and designer Peter Gee
Sprachzertifikat | Language Certificate "Chamber of Commerce"
Vierwöchiger Kurs an der „Cherry Marshall Model School", Bond Street | four-weeks course at "Cherry Marshall Model School", Bond Street
Einwöchiger Kurs „Colour and Modern Art" an einer Kunstschule in Oxfordshire | one-week course "Colour and Modern Art" at an art school in Oxfordshire
Besuch der Abendschule „Basic Design" von Peter Gee, London | visits the evening school "Basic Design" run by Peter Gee, London
Teilzeitstudentin im Schmuckdepartment der Central School of Arts (heute Central Saint Martins College of Art and Design) | part-time student at the Precious Jewellery Department at Central School of Arts (Central Saint Martins College of Art and Design)
Privatschule für „Basic Labours and Shapers" | private school for "Basic Labours and Shapers"

1959
Unterricht in Modern Dance bei Ernst Berk | studies in Modern Dance with Ernst Berk

1960
Paris, Frankreich | France
Besucht private Kunstschule für Zeichnen und Design | studies at private art school for drawing and design
Unterricht in Modern Dance bei Jerome Andrews | studies in Modern Dance with Jerome Andrews
Ferienkurs bei Victor Pasmore, Colchester | summer course with Victor Pasmore, Colchester

1961
Belegt „Foundation, Form and Colour Studies" am Leeds College of Art bei Victor Pasmore und Harry Thubron | studies "Foundation, Form and Colour Studies" with Victor Pasmore and Harry Thubron at Leeds College of Art

1962
Wunsch, in Pforzheim Schmuck zu studieren | wishes to study jewelry in Pforzheim
Beteiligung mit Schmuckarbeiten an Ausstellung der Central School

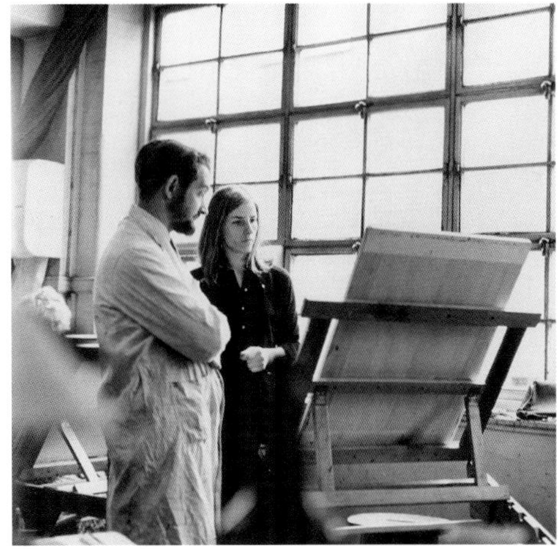

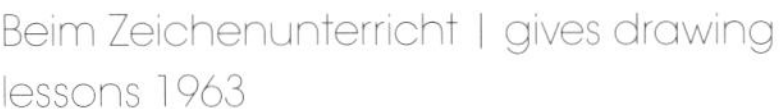

Beim Zeichenunterricht | gives drawing lessons 1963

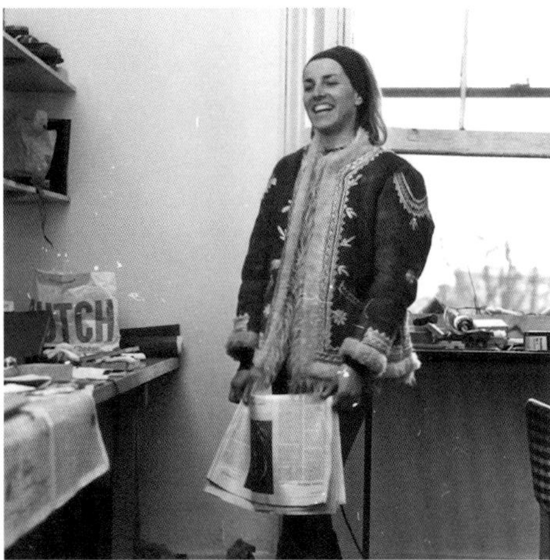

London 1967

of Arts, London (heute Central Saint Martins College of Art and Design) | pieces of jewelry shown at exhibition Central School of Arts, London (today Central Saint Martins College of Art and Design)

1963

Kennenlernen von Eduardo Guedes, Student in einer Filmklasse in Leicester | meets Eduardo Guedes, student of a film class in Leicester

Lehrerlaubnis für Großbritannien | teaching permit for Great Britain

Geschäft in Central London verkauft Schmuck von Helga Zahn | shop in Central London is selling Helga Zahn's jewelry

1962–1964

Unterrichtet drei Tage in der Woche im Kurs „Foundation, Form and Colour" unter Leitung von Tom Hudson am Leicester College of Arts | three days a week teacher of the course "Foundation, Form and Colour" supervised by Tom Hudson

1964

Adresse | address: Upper Park Road, London-Hampstead

1965

Sommerkurs „Basic Research 65" in New York, unterrichtet gemeinsam mit Peter Gee und Thomas M. Messer | summer course "Basic Research 65" in New York, teaches in collaboration with Peter Gee and Thomas M. Messer

Abhaltung eines Sommerkurses unter Leitung von Robert Hedley Lewis am Coventry Art College | teacher of a summer course supervised by Robert Hedley Lewis at Coventry Art College

Assistentin von James Burr am City Literarture Institute, London | assists James Burr at City Literature Institute, London

1966

Goldmedaille des Bayerischen Staatspreises, überreicht auf der Internationalen Handwerksmesse München | Gold Medal of the Bavarian State awarded during the Internationale Handwerksmesse München

1967

Studio in St. Giles Passage, Charing Cross Road, London

Unterrichtet an der Haystack School of Arts, Deer Isle, MA, USA (Sommerschule) | teaches at Haystack School of Arts,Deer Isle, MA, USA (summer school)

Arbeit an Siebdrucken im Studio von Peter Gee, New York | workes on silkcreens at the studio of Peter Gee, New York

Schmuckarbeiten gezeigt auf Fashionshow von Modedesigner Tzaims Luksus, New York | jewelry works are presented during fashion show of fashion designer Tzaims Luksus, New York

1970

Gemeinsam mit Eduardo Guedes Arbeit an dem Experimental-Kurzfilm „We Hope to Paint it Blue", Erstaufführung auf der Eröffnungsveranstaltung der Hofer Filmtage | collaborates with Eduardo Guedes on the experimental film "We Hope to Paint it Blue", first shown at the opening of the Hofer Filmtage

1972

Teilnahme am Internationalen Schmuckwettbewerb „Ansteckschmuck", Schmuckmuseum Pforzheim | participates in the International Jewelry Competition "Ansteckschmuck", Schmuckmuseum Pforzheim

1973

Stellt Victor Ely als Mitarbeiter für Schmuck ein | employes Victor Ely as an assistant for jewelry

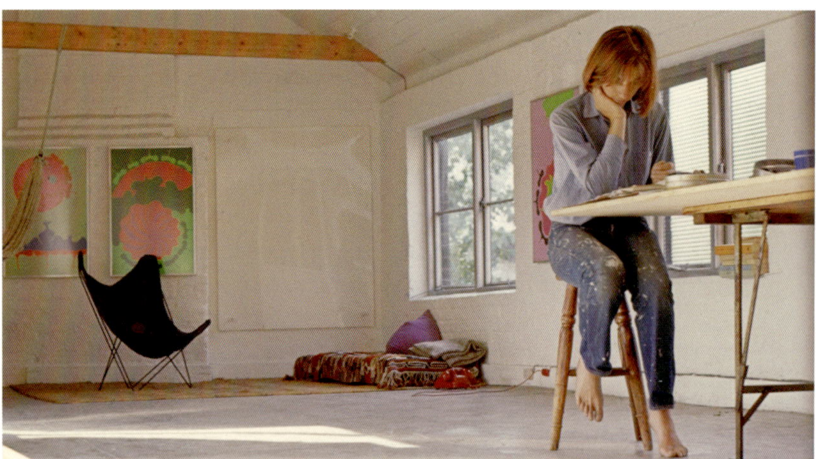

Studio 1964

1974–1976
Dozentin am Hornsey College of Art, Middlesex Polytechnikum in der Abteilung Schmuck, London I instructor at the jewelry department of Hornsey College of Art, Middlesex Polytechnic, London
1976
Stellt Praktikantin für Schmuck ein I employes an intern for jewelry
1978
Sommerkurs für Goldschmiede bei Bruno Martinazzi in Ansedonia, Italien I summer course for goldsmiths with Bruno Martinazzi in Ansedonia, Italy
1979
Studiert Emaillieren, Löten, Cloisonné an der Kulicke-Starck Academy of Jewelry Art, New York I studies in enamel, soldering, cloisonné at Kulicke-Starck Academy of Jewelry, New York
26.10.1985
Helga Zahn stirbt auf Stromboli, Italien I Helga Zahn passes away on Stromboli, Italy

Auszeichnungen I awards

1966
Goldmedaille des Bayerischen Staatspreises, überreicht auf der Internationalen Handwerksmesse München I Gold Medal of the Bavarian State awarded during the Internationale Handwerksmesse München
1975
Stipendium I Bursary of Crafts Advisory Committee, London

Einzelausstellungen I solo exhibitions

1965
Design Research Inc., New York, USA (jewelry)
1966
Helga Zahn – Jewellery and silkscreens. Axiom Gallery, London, Great Britain
1968
Helga Zahn. Kollagen, Gemälde und Siebdrucke. Schmuckmuseum Pforzheim, Germany (graphics, paintings)
1969
ApoGee Studio, New York, USA (jewelry and silkscreens)
Jewellery by Helga Zahn. Nicholas Treadwell Gallery, London, Great Britain (jewelry and silkscreens)
1970
Galerie Richard Foncke, Ghent, Belgium (jewelry, paintings, silkscreens)
Helga Zahn. Collagen – Grafik – Zeichnungen. Galerie Weinelt (Bootshaus), Hof, Germany (paintings, silkscreens)
Helga Zahn. Schmuck und Juwelierarbeiten. Boutique Bijou, Hof, Germany (jewelry)
1974
Jewellery by Helga Zahn. National Museum Wales, Cardiff, Great Brittain
1976
Helga Zahn. A Retrospective Assessment 1960–1976. Jewellery, Prints and Drawings. Crafts Advisory Committee, London, Great Britain **(S. I p. 98)**
1978
Galerie Obelisk, Boston, USA (jewelry)
1990
Helga Zahn. Schmuck-Design. Heimatmuseum Traunreut, Germany (jewelry, paintings, silkscreens)
2016
Helga Zahn. Schmuck. Unikat und Serie. Kunstgalerie Altes Rathaus, Schwarzenbach a. d. Saale, Germany (jewelry, silkscreens)

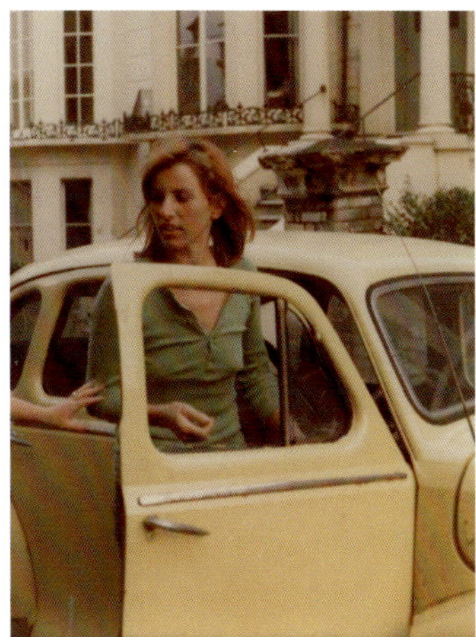

London 1967

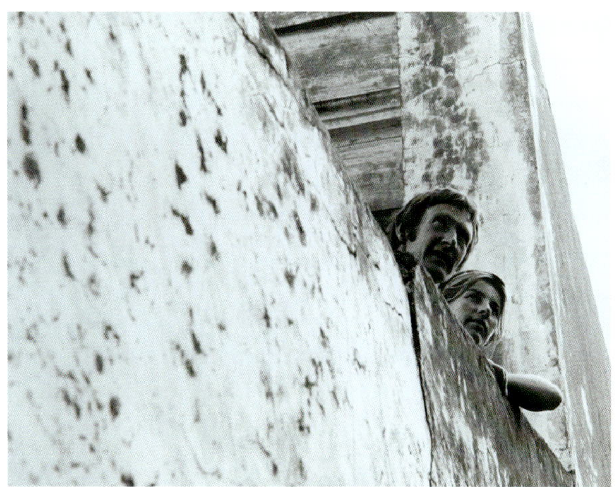

Mit Peter Gee auf Stromboli | with Peter Gee on Stromboli island, 1970

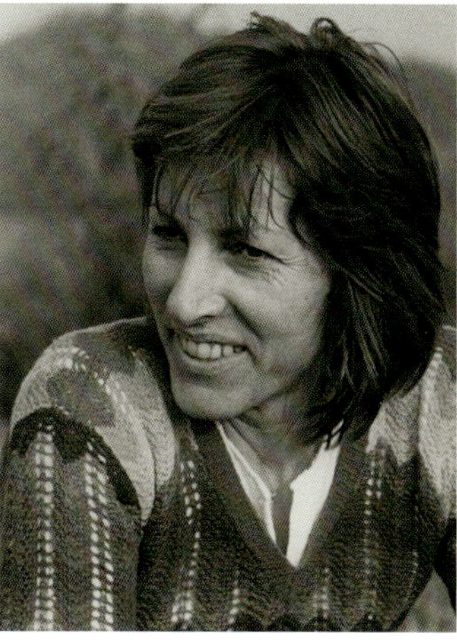

In den 1980er-Jahren | in the 1980s

Ausstellungsbeteiligungen | participation in group exhibitions

1965
New End Gallery, London, Great Britain (jewelry)
Jewellery 65. Ewan Philipps Gallery, London, Great Britain (jewelry)

1966
Internationale Handwerksmesse München, Germany (jewelry)
British Week. Milan, Italy (jewelry)
Design Research Inc., New York, USA (jewelry)
Design Centre, London, Great Britain (jewelry)
The Goldsmith Today. Goldsmiths' Hall, London, Great Britain (jewelry)
Christmas Exhibition. Crafts Center London, Great Britain (jewelry)
Wanderausstellung | touring exhibition Worshipful Company of Goldsmiths, USA and Canada (jewelry)

1967
The Scottish Design Center, Glasgow, Great Britain (jewelry)
Fashion Show Tzaims Luksus, New York, USA (jewelry)

1968
Internationale Schmuckausstellung „Jablonec '68", Czechoslovakia (jewelry)
Bear Lane Gallery, Oxford, Great Britain (jewelry and silkscreens)
The Goldsmith Today. Goldsmiths' Hall, London, Great Britain (jewelry)

1969
Development of Modern Jewellery. PACE Gallery, London, Great Britain (jewelry),
Bloomingdales, London, Great Britain (jewelry)
Liverpool Building & Design Center, Liverpool, Great Britain (jewelry)
Obelisk Gallery, Boston, USA (jewelry)
Barharbour Gallery, Maine, USA (jewelry)
Galerie Heseler, München, Germany (silkscreens?)

1970
Schmuck 70 – Tendenzen. Schmuckmuseum, Pforzheim, Germany (jewelry)
Christmas Exhibition of Glass, Sculpture and Jewellery. Queens Square Gallery, Leeds, Great Britain (jewelry)

1971
Contemporary jewellery. D.L.I. Museum & Arts Centre, Durham, Great Britain
Opening Exhibition Electrum Gallery. London, Great Britain (jewelry) **(S. | p. 100)**
Christmas at Electrum. London, Great Britain (jewelry)
Christmas Exhibition of Jewellery. Queens Square Gallery, Leeds, Great Britain

1972
Sierraad 1900–1972. Zonnehof, Amersfoort, Netherlands (jewelry)
Camden 72. Swiss Cottage Library, London, Great Britain (jewelry)
Park Square Gallery Ltd., Leeds, Great Britain (jewelry)
Exhibition on the occasion of Internationaler Schmuckwettbewerb „Ansteckschmuck". Schmuckmuseum Pforzheim, Germany (jewelry)

1973
The Craftsman's Art. CAC exhibition at the Victoria & Albert Museum, London, Great Britain (jewelry)
British Jewellery. Goldschmiedehaus Hanau, Germany, in cooperation with Electrum Gallery, Royal College of Art, Central School of Art and Middlesex Politechnic, London, Great Britain (jewelry)
Aspects of Jewellery. Aberdeen Art Gallery, Scotland, in coopera-

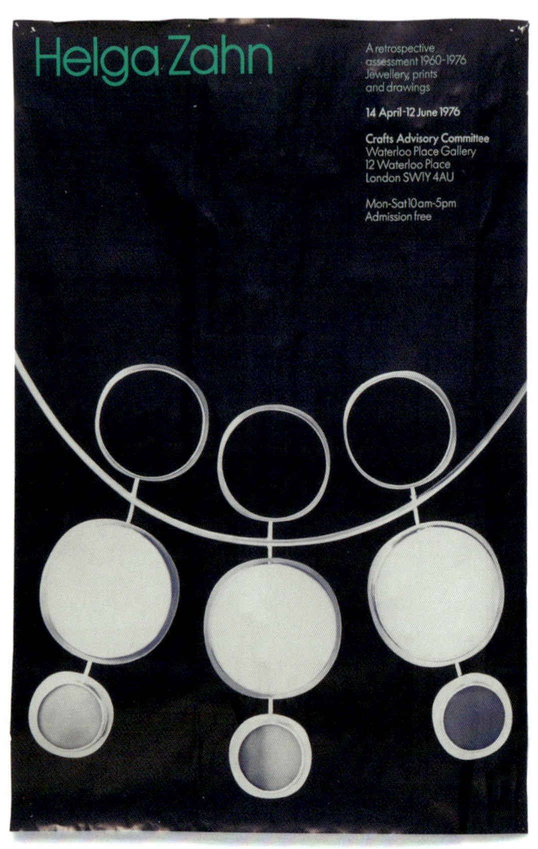
Helga Zahn
A retrospective
assessment 1960-1976
Jewellery, prints
and drawings
14 April-12 June 1976
Crafts Advisory Committee
Waterloo Place Gallery
12 Waterloo Place
London SW1Y 4AU
Mon-Sat 10am-5pm
Admission free
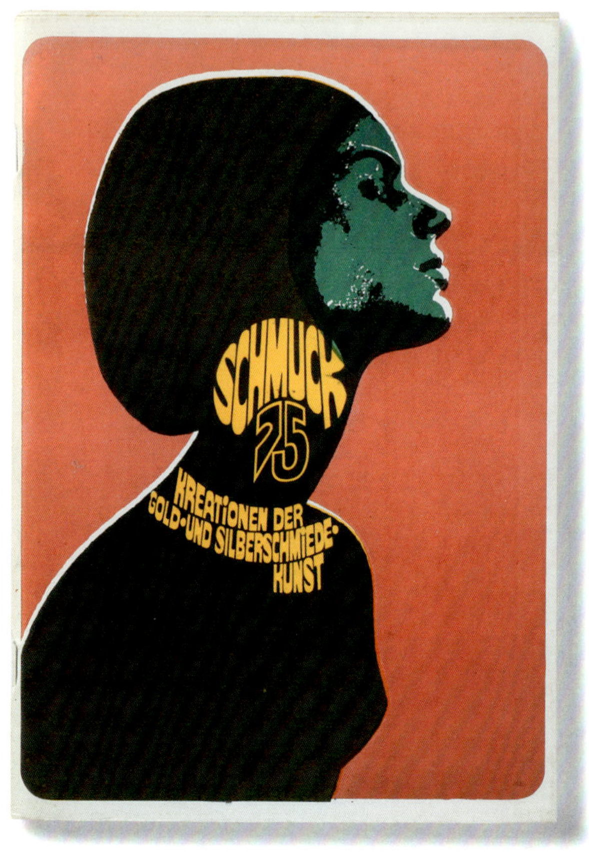
SCHMUCK
75
KREATIONEN DER
GOLD- UND SILBERSCHMIEDE-
KUNST

tion with Electrum Gallery, London, Great Britain (jewelry)
Graves Gallery, Sheffield, Great Britain (silkscreens)
1975
Schmuck '75. Eberli & Fischer Gallery, Gottlieben, Switzerland (jewelry / **S. I p. 98)**
D.L.I. Museum & Arts Center, Durham, Great Britain (jewelry)
1975/1976
Wanderausstellung | touring exhibition: Jewellery in Europe. Scottish Arts Council / Crafts Advisory Committee Exhibition, Edinburgh, Victoria & Albert Museum, London, Great Britain (jewelry)
1978
Crafts Council Collection Display. Casel Museum, Norwich, Great Britain (jewelry)
1979
Galerie Petri, Hof, Germany (jewelry)
1980
Westdean Cottage, Eduard James Foundation, Farnham, Surrey, Great Britain (jewelry)
Schmuck International. International Jewellery 1900–1980. Künstlerhaus Wien, Austria (jewelry)
Walsall Museum, Walsall, Great Britain (jewelry)
1980/1981
Wanderausstellung | touring exhibition: David Cripps – Photography. Crafts Advisory Committee London, Great Britain (photos of jewelry)
1981
"Crafts Advisory Collection Display", Stoke-on-Trent, Great Britain (jewelry)
1982
Oxfordshire Museum Service, Woodstock, Oxfordshire, Great Britain (jewelry)
Makers Eye. Crafts Advisory Committee, London, Great Britain (jewelry)
seit | since 1986
Ständige Ausstellung | permanent exhibition Crafts Council London, Great Britain (jewelry)
1991
20th Anniversary Exhibition. Electrum Gallery London, Great Britain (jewelry)
1995
Moderne Schmuckkunst, veranstaltet vom Schmuckmuseum Pforzheim, Germany, Ethnographisches Museum, St. Petersburg, Russland | International Jewelry Exhibition, organized by Schmuckmuseum Pforzheim, Germany, Russian Museum of Ethnography, St. Petersburg, Russia (jewelry)
2001
Het Versierde Ego. Het Kunstjuweel in de 20ste eeuw / The Ego Adorned. 20th Century Artists' Jewellery. Antwerpen, Belgium
seit | since 2010
Ständige Ausstellung | permanent exhibition Die Neue Sammlung/ Danner Rotunde, Pinakothek der Moderne, Munich, Germany (jewelry)
2015
A Sense of Jewellery. Goldsmiths' Center, London, Great Britain (jewelry)
2016
I Am Here. Portable Art, Wearable Objects, Jewellery since the 1970s. Crafts Council Exhibition, Upper Gulbenkian Gallery at the Royal College of Art, London, Great Britain (jewelry)

Schmuckarbeiten in öffentlichen Institutionen | jewelry works in public collections

Staatliche Museen Berlin – Kunstgewerbemuseum
The National Museum of Wales, Cardiff
Museum Angewandte Kunst, Frankfurt
Museum für Kunst und Gewerbe, Hamburg
Crafts Council, London
Goldsmiths' Hall, London
Victoria & Albert Museum, London
Die Neue Sammlung – The Design Museum, Munich
Die Neue Sammlung – The Design Museum. Permanent Loan of Danner Foundation Munich
Schmuckmuseum Pforzheim
Collection West Sussex College of Art, Worthing

Buchgestaltung | book design

Jerzy Niemojowski. Gedichte, 1963 West Sussex College of Design, Worthing, o.A.
Klares Lewes. Jewellery Making for the Animator. Batsford, London 1965
Ausst.-Kat. | exh. cat. Fotoausstellung des Romans „La Femme 100 Têtes" von Max Ernst (1929), 1968 (?)
Ausst.-Kat. | exh. cat. Helga Zahn. Kollagen, Gemälde und Siedrucke. Schmuckmuseum Pforzheim, 1968
Ausst.-Kat. | exh. cat. Electrum Gallery, London 1971

Plakate und Druckgrafik | posters and prints

John Lloyd Bookshop, Wimbledon
Crafts Centre of Great Britain, London (Plakat, Briefkopf, Visitenkarte | poster, letterhead, business card)
Théâtre des Nations, Paris, 1969 (Plakat, Jahresprogramm | poster, annual)
Papierfabrik, Paris, 1969 (Plakate | posters)
Arnel television network campaign, USA (Plakate | posters)

Film

Experimentalfilm „We Hope to Paint it Blue" mit Eduardo Guedes, Erstaufführung Hof 1970 | experimental film "We Hope to Paint it Blue" in cooperation with Eduardo Guedes, first run Hof 1970
"Beat of Brazil", British United Airways (titles)

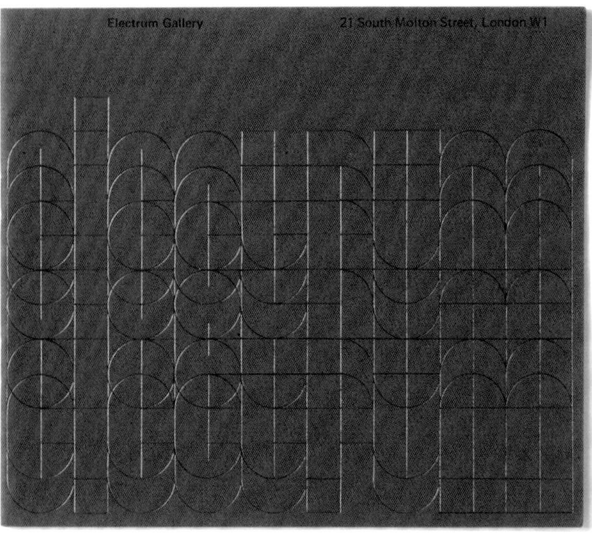

Television programs, Warner Brothers / Seven Artists (graphics and titles)

Ausstellungsdesign | exhibition design

Fotoausstellung des Romans „La Femme 100 Têtes" von Max Ernst (1929), 1968 (?)
Christmas exhibition, Crafts Center of Great Britain, London, Great Britain 1971
Eröffnungsausstellung | opening exhibition Gallery Electrum, London, Great Britain 1971 (jewelry)
AIGA, New York, USA
ApoGee Studio, New York, USA

Auswahlbibliographie | selected bibliography

1963
Tatler Magazin, January 1963
1964
Joys and pitfalls in freelance design. In: Hampstead & Highgate Express and Hampstead Garden Suburb and Golders Green News, July 17th, 1964
1965
Klares Lewes. Jewelry Making for the amateur. London, New York 1965
K.-H. Sch. (Übersetzung). Als Künstlerin in London. Kunstschaffen einer Schwarzenbacherin anerkannt. In: Zeitung Schwarzenbach, 1965
1966
Goldmedaillen für die Handwerksarbeit. Wirtschaftsminister Schedl überreichte auf der Handwerksmesse die Staatspreise – 30 Aussteller wurden ausgezeichnet, in: o. A. (Archiv Helga Zahn)
Kleine Chronik unserer Stadt. In: Schwarzenbacher Amtsblatt, Frühjahr 1966
1968
Helga Zahn. Begleitheft zur Ausstellung „Helga Zahn. Siebdrucke, Kollagen und Gemälde" im Schmuckmuseum Pforzheim mit einem Beitrag von Gene Baro, London 1968 (Eigenverlag)
Magazijn „De Bijenkorf", Amsterdam, 25.11.1968
Internationale Bijouterieausstellung Jablonec nad Nisou. In: Uhren und Schmuck, 1968, 12, S. 360 (Abb.)
1969
W. Wie. Ausstellung Schwarzenbacher Maler. In: Frankenpost, 24. Juli 1969
1970
Ausst.-Kat. | exh. cat. Schmuck '70 Tendenzen. Schmuckmuseum Pforzheim 1970, o. S.
SZ. Eine Freude für das Auge. In London lebende Hoferin stellt Bilder und Juwelierarbeiten vor. In: Hofer Anzeiger / Frankenpost, Nr. 138, 10.06.1970.
Kulturwarte, Juni 1970 (Experimentalfilm)
G. Hertel. Zwei Richter setzen das Maß. In: Hofer Anzeiger, 21. Juli 1970
1971
Dem Bootshaus folgt Kunst … In: Hofer Anzeiger, 7. Mai 1971
1973
Ausst.-Kat. | exh. cat. British Jewellery. Deutsches Goldschmiedehaus Hanau in Zusammenarbeit mit der Electrum Galerie , sowie dem Royal College of Art, der Central School of Art und dem Middlesex Polytechnic London, Hanau 1973, o. S.
Ausst.-Kat. | exh. cat. Aspects of Jewellery by contributors from Electrum Gallery, Aberdeen Art Gallery, Aberdeen 1973, o. S.
1974
J. Anderson Black. A History of Jewels. New York 1974
1975
Helga Zahn. In: Gold + Silber, Mai 1975, Nr. 5, o. S.
Helga Zahn. Jeweller. In: Crafts, May/June 1975, Nr. 14, S. 10

Ralph Turner (?). Helga Zahn. In: Crafts, July/August 1975, Nr. 15, S. 24–27
Ausst.-Kat. | exh. cat. Schmuck '75. Kreationen der Gold- und Silberschmiedekunst. Galerie Eberli + Fischer, Gottlieben 1975 **(S. | p. 98)**

1976

Ausst.-Kat. | exh. cat. A Retrospective Assessment 1960–1976. Jewellery, Prints and Drawings. Crafts Advisory Committee, London 1976 (exhibition officer: Ralph Turner, **S. | p. 98**)
Ausst.-Kat. | exh. cat. An Exibition of Progressive Work. Selected by Ralph Turner. The Scottish Arts Council Gallery, Edinburgh / The Victoria & Albert Museum, London / Aberdeen Art Gallery & Museum, Aberdeen / Third Eye Centre, Glasgow / Arnolfini Gallery, Bristol, Edinburgh 1976
Ralph Turner. Contemporary Jewelry. A Critical Assessment 1945–1975. London 1976, S. 5, 53–54, 74, 124-125, 193

1980

Ausst.-Kat. | exh. cat. Schmuck International. 1900–1980 Künstlerhaus Wien, Wien 1980, S. 181–182, 239
Schmuckmuseum Pforzheim. Von der Antike bis zur Gegenwart. Pforzheim 1980, S. 375 (Nr. 372)

1983

Jewelry. Undifened. In: Crafts. No. 61. March/April 1983. S. 38, 42

1985

Caroline Broadhead. New Traditions. The Evolution of Jewellery 1966–1985. London 1985, S. 10, 81
Peter Dormer / Ralph Turner. The New Jewelry: Trends and Traditions. London 1985, S. 16

1986

Ralph Turner. Helga Zahn. In: Crafts, Jan./Febr. 1986, Nr. 78, S. 11
Peter Dormer / Ralph Turner. Schmuck. Die Internationale Avantgarde. Ideen – Stile – Tendenzen. Köln 1986, S. 12

1990

Ausst.-Kat. | exh. cat. Helga Zahn. Schmuck-Design. Hrsg. Klaus Zahn, Heimathaus Traunreut 1990 (Eigenverlag)
P. S. Silberschmuck als Hommage an die Diana. In: Traunreuter Anzeiger, 1990 (Archiv Helga Zahn)
Ein „Ereignis" im Traunreuter Heimathaus. Heute eröffnet eine bemerkenswerte Ausstellung von Schmuck, Malerei und Graphik. In: Traunreuter Anzeiger, 1990 (Archiv Helga Zahn)
J. Bader. Aufruf zur Verschönerung des Denkens. Ausstellung von Günther Schuhböck und Helga Zahn im Traunreuter Heimathaus. In: Traunsteiner Wochenblatt, 24.10.1990
Franz Maier. Großer Auftakterfolg im Heimathaus. 200 Gäste kamen zur Vernissage der Ausstellung Helga Zahn und Günther Schuhböck. In: Traunreuter Stadtnachrichten, 20.10.1990

1994

Peter Dormer / Ralph Turner. The New Jewelry. Trends and Traditions. London 1994 (Revised Edition, first edition 1984), S. 12, 210

1996

Ausst.-Kat. | exh. cat. Ralph Turner. Jewelry in Europe and America. New Times, New Thinking. Crafts Council Gallery, London 1996, S. 18, 20, 50, 82, 137

1998

Fritz Falk / Cornelie Holzach. Schmuck der Moderne. Modern Jewellery 1960–1998. Stuttgart 1999, S. 25, 46, 223

2001

Ausst.-Kat. | exh. cat. Het Versierde Ego. Het Kunstjuweel in de 20ste eeuw / The Ego Adorned. 20th Century Artists' Jewellery. Hrsg. v. Jan Walgrave, Konigin Fabiolazaal, Antwerpen 2001, S. 113–114

2010

Benno und Therese Danner'sche Kunstgewerbestiftung (Hrsg.). Danner Stiftung. Tätigkeitsbericht 2010, München 2010
Knochen und Kiesel in der Pinakothek der Moderne. Schmuck aus Naturmaterialien und feinsten Edelsteinen von Helga Zahn. o. A. 10./11. April 2010, S. 17 (Archiv Helga Zahn)
Sh. Eine Würdigung ihrer Arbeit. Designer-Schmuck von Helga Zahn ist in der Pinakothek der Moderne in München zu bestaunen. In: Schwarzenbacher Amtsblatt, 30. April 2010
Ausstellungen am Wochenende. In: Traunreuter Anzeiger, 30. April–1./2. Mai 2010

2011

Clare Phillips. Jewels & Jewellery. London 2011 (Erstausgabe 2000, revidierte Neuauflage 2008)

2015

Ausst.-Kat. | exh. cat. A Sense of Jewellery. Goldsmiths' Center, London 2015
Ausst. Kat. | exh. cat. I Am Here. Portable art, wearable objects, jewellery sinnce the 1970s. Crafts Council touring exhibition. London 2015

2016

Ausst.-Kat. | exh. cat. Helga Zahn. Schmuck. Unikat und Serie. Jewelry. One-Off and series. Kunstgalerie Altes Rathaus Schwarzenbach a. d. Saale, Stuttgart 2016
Beatriz Chadour-Sampson, Janice Hosegood. Barbara Cartlidge and Electrum Gallery. A Passion for Jewellery, Stuttgart 2016, S. 63, 96, 264-267, 273

Textnachweise | Notes

1 „Helga Zahn war in dieser Zeit in Großbritannien für den Schmuck eine wichtige befreiende Kraft … Sie beklagte zwar oft die zeitraubenden Arbeitsprozesse der Goldschmiede und ihre lähmende Wirkung auf die künstlerische Spontaneität, dennoch begnügte sie sich nie mit einem Kompromiss, was nicht zuletzt ihre großartigen Arbeiten belegen." In: Ralph Turner. Jewellery in Europe. New Times. New Thinking. London 1996, S. 50.
2 Zeitungsartikel: „Goldmedaillen für die Handwerksarbeit. Wirtschaftsminister Schedl übereichte auf der Handwerksmesse die Staatspreise – 30 Aussteller wurden ausgezeichnet", 1966 o. A. (Archiv Helga Zahn). | Newspaper article: "Gold medals for handcrafted works. Minister of Economics Schedl presented the State Awards at the arts and crafts trade fair – 30 exhibitors received awards" (trans.), no author stated, Helga Zahn Archive.
3 Ausst.-Kat. | Exh. cat. Helga Zahn. Schmuck-Design. Hrsg. von Klaus Zahn, Traunreut, 1990, S. 7.
4 Brief an die Eltern, 05.01.1962, Archiv Helga Zahn. | Letter to her parents, Jan. 5, 1962, Helga Zahn Archive.
5 Hampstead and Highland Express, 17.07.1964. Zusammengefasst in: Als Künstlerin in London. Kunstschaffen einer Schwarzenbacherin anerkannt. Übersetzt von K. H. Sch., o. A., Archiv Helga Zahn. | translated by K. H. Sch. Helga Zahn Archive.
6 Brief an Eduardo Guedes, 23.12.1964, Archiv Helga Zahn. | Letter to Eduardo Guedes, Dec. 23, 1964, Helga Zahn Archive.
7 Brief an Eduardo Guedes, 18.12.1964, Archiv Helga Zahn. | Letter to Eduardo Guedes, Dec. 18, 1964, Helga Zahn Archive.
8 Wendy Ramshaw, in: Ausst.-Kat. | Exh. cat. Helga Zahn. Schmuck-Design. Hrsg. von Klaus Zahn, Traunreut, 1990, S. 5.
9 Beschriftung auf der Rückseite eines Fotos, Archiv Helga Zahn. | Writing on the back of a photograph, Helga Zahn Archive.
10 Brief an die Mutter, Dez. 1967, Archiv Helga Zahn. | Letter to her mother, Dec. 1967, Helga Zahn Archive.
11 Brief an die Mutter, 18.03.1969, Archiv Helga Zahn. | Letter to her mother, March 18, 1969, Helga Zahn Archive.
12 Internationale Bijouterieausstellung Jablonec nad Nisou. In: Uhren und Schmuck, 1968, 12, S. 360 (Abb.).
13 Einladungskarte zur Ausstellung, Archiv Helga Zahn. | Invitation to the exhibition, Helga Zahn Archive.
14 Brief an die Mutter, 27.04.1969, Archiv Helga Zahn. | Letter to her mother, April 27, 1969, Helga Zahn Archive.
15 Brief an die Mutter, 17. Nov. 1969, Archiv Helga Zahn. | Letter to her mother, Nov. 17, 1969, Helga Zahn Archive.
16 W. Wie: Ausstellung Schwarzenbacher Maler. In: Frankenpost, 24. Juli. 1969.
17 G. Hertel: Zwei Richter setzen das Maß. In: Hofer Anzeiger, 21. Juli 1970.
18 Mündliche Mitteilung von Kerstin Weinelt am 28.06.2016. | As told by Kerstin Weinelt on June 28, 2016.
19 Mündliche Mitteilung von Elisabeth und Klaus Zahn am 17.05.2016. | As told by Elisabeth and Klaus Zahn on May 17, 2016.
20 E-Mail von Ray Carpenter, 08.06.2016. | Email from Ray Carpenter dated June 8, 2016.
21 Brief, 28.04.1973, Archiv Helga Zahn. | Letter, April 28, 1973, Helga Zahn Archive.
22 Wendy Ramshaw in: Ausst.-Kat. Helga Zahn. Schmuck-Design. Hrsg. von Klaus Zahn, Traunreut, S. 5.
23 Brief, 02.11.1974, Archiv Helga Zahn. | Letter, Nov. 2, 1974, Helga Zahn Archive.
24 Crafts Magazine, Juli/August 1975, S. 24.
25 "I've been buying a lot of jewelry designed by artists. As a matter of fact, I don't have jewels. And this I enjoyed. I wear them …". In: Oral history interview with Vera List, 1973, Jan. 9; Archives of American Art, www.aaa.si.edu/collections/interviews/oral-history-interview-vera-list, 18.06.2016.
26 Brief, 27.04.1976, Archiv Helga Zahn. | Letter, April 27, 1976, Helga Zahn Archive.
27 Ausst.-Kat. | Exh. cat. Loot. An exhibition of new gold, silver, jewels, glass and medals for sale at under £50 with a section £50 – £100. Hrsg. v. Worshipful Company of Goldsmiths, London 1976, o. S.
28 Brief, 04.08.1978, Archiv Helga Zahn. | Letter, Aug. 4, 1978, Helga Zahn Archive.

29 E-mail von Peter Skubic, 04.04.2016 I E-mail by Peter Skubic, April 4, 2016

30 „Helga Zahns Arbeiten waren sehr wichtig für mich. Ich sah ihre Strenge und ihre Vision in ihren Stücken. Ich sah die schöne Anordnung und das Formale ihrer Entwürfe. Ihre technischen Fähigkeiten waren nicht ausgereift, aber das brauchten sie auch nicht zu sein. Helga Zahn arbeitete mit einem hohen Anspruch an sich selbst: sorgfältig und vorsichtig die Balance und Struktur der einzelnen Teile zueinander auslotend, um am Ende große Formen aus Silber entstehen zu lassen." Wendy Ramshaw, in: Ausst.-Kat. Helga Zahn. Schmuck-Design. Heimathaus. Hrsg. v. Klaus Zahn. Traunreut 1990, S. 7.

31 „Helga Zahns Arbeiten waren gemildert modern, unprätentiös, klar, sinnlich und menschlich. In den Niederlanden standen ganz andere Fragen im Bereich Schmuck zu der Zeit an. Die Erneuerungstendenzen waren extrem interessant, doch entfernte sich gleichzeitig der Schmuck vom Träger, dieser physisch anwesenden, denkenden und sozialen Person. Deshalb versuche ich heute den Menschen stärker in meiner eigenen Kunst zu berücksichtigen. Deshalb schätze ich das Werk von Helga Zahn mehr und mehr und sehe sie als eine der wichtigsten Pionierinnen und Künstlerinnen im Autorenschmuck an", E-Mail von Paul Derrez, Schmuckkünstler und Eigentümer Galerie RA, Amsterdam, 04.08.2016

32 "...the 'Cool Aunt Helga' with the reddish colored smooth long hair and long dark red or dark purple baggy velvet dresses"; E-mail by Tine Waldenfels, niece, 29.04.2016

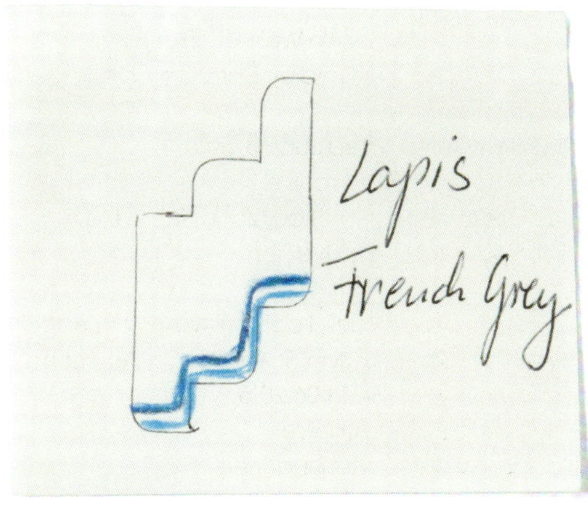

Schnittschablone „Lapis, French Grey"
cutting stencil "Lapis, French Grey", 1968/1971
Papier, Kugelschreiber, Buntstift | paper, ballpoint pen, crayon
H. 5,7 cm, B. 6,7 cm | h. 5,7 cm, w. 6,7 cm
Die Neue Sammlung – The Design Museum

Die vorliegende Publikation erscheint anlässlich der Ausstellung „Helga Zahn. Schmuck. Unikat und Serie", Kunstgalerie Altes Rathaus Schwarzenbach a. d. Saale vom 24.09.–6.11.2016 und Die Neue Sammlung – The Design Museum im Frühjahr 2019.
The book is published on the occasion of the exhibition "Helga Zahn. Schmuck. Unikat und Serie. Jewelry. One-Off and series.", Kunstgalerie Altes Rathaus Schwarzenbach a. d. Saale 24.09.–6.11.2016 and Die Neue Sammlung – The Design Museum in spring 2019.

Herausgeber | Editors
Stadt Schwarzenbach a. d. Saale,
Die Neue Sammlung – The Design Museum
Katalogkonzept | Catalog concept
Petra Hölscher (Die Neue Sammlung)
Autoren | Authors
Petra Hölscher, Helga Zahn
Mitarbeit | Assistances
Die Neue Sammlung:
Daniela Augstein (DA), Nadine Engel, Evamaria Lösche (EL), Maja Schmidt (MS)
Stadt Schwarzenbach:
Barbara Muck, Sabine Oltsch
Fotografien (soweit nicht anders bezeichnet) | **Photographs** (unless otherwise stated)
Alexander Laurenzo (Die Neue Sammlung)
Übersetzung | Translation
Jeremy Gaines
Redaktion | Editorial staff
Petra Hölscher
Lektorat | Copy editing
Nadine Engel, Petra Hölscher, Sabine Klinkert (Die Neue Sammlung)
Grafische Gestaltung | Layout
Swanti Bräsecke-Bartsch

Druck | Print
Förster & Borries GmbH & Co. KG, Zwickau
Papier | Paper
Amber Graphic 120/150 g/qm, Allegro 150 g/qm

Seite 1 | page 1
Ring | ring, 1968; Silber | silver
H. 4,5 cm, B. 3,2 cm, T. 0,6 cm | h. 4,5 cm, w. 3,2 cm, d. 0,6 cm

Die Neue Sammlung – The Design Museum. Dauerleihgabe der Danner-Stiftung München | permanent loan of the Danner Foundation Munich
Frontespiz | Frontispiece
Helga Zahn in London, 1962
Foto: Archiv Helga Zahn
Biografie | biographie
Fotos: Archiv Helga Zahn

Eine Ausstellung der Kunstgalerie Altes Rathaus in Schwarzenbach a. d. Saale und der Neuen Sammlung – The Design Museum.
An exhibition of Kunstgalerie Altes Rathaus in Schwarzenbach a. d. Saale and of Die Neue Sammlung – The Design Museum.

Kurator | Curator
Petra Hölscher (Die Neue Sammlung)
Ausstellungskonzeption | Exhibition concept
Petra Hölscher
Ausstellungsorganisation | Exhibition organization
Petra Hölscher, Barbara Muck (Kunstgalerie Schwarzenbach a. d. Saale)
Restauratorische Betreuung | Conservation Department
Tim Bechthold, Helene Ernst (Die Neue Sammlung)
Museumstechnik | Technical Department
Die Neue Sammlung:
Cornelius von Heyking, Toni Baumann
Stadt Schwarzenbach: Reinhold Barthold und Mitarbeiter, Andreas Vogel
Presse- und Öffentlichkeitsarbeit für die Ausstellung | Press and public realtions for the exhibition in:
Kunstgalerie Altes Rathaus in Schwarzenbach:
Petra Hölscher, Barbara Muck, Sabine Oltsch
Die Neue Sammlung – The Design Museum:
Tine Nehler, Jette Elixmann

Unser Dank gebührt | Thanks to
Hans-Peter Baumann, Schwarzenbach a. d. Saale
Caroline Broadhead, London
Claus Bury, Frankfurt
Ray Carpenter, London
Beatriz Chadour, London
Paul Derrez, Amsterdam
Sabina Eckenfels, Schmuckmuseum Pforzheim
Odil Gee, New York
Thomas Gentille, New York
Alexandra Hentschel, Schwarzenbach a. d. Saale
Rainer Hübsch, Hof
Cornelie Holzach, Schmuckmuseum Pforzheim
Paul Lemieux, New York
Fritz Maierhofer, Wien
Mitglieder Arbeitskreis Bildende Kunst im Kulturverein Schwarzenbach a. d. Saale
Manfred Petri, München
Ulrich Pohlmann, München
Georgia Powell, The Goldsmiths' Company, London
Sabine Runde, Museum Angewandte Kunst Frankfurt
Peter Skubic, Gamischdorf
Hans Stofer, London
Christine Waidenschlager, Staatliche Museen Berlin – Kunstgewerbemuseum
Christine Walther, Hof
David Watkins, London
Elizabeth Wratislav, Crafts Council, London
sowie allen genannten und ungenannt bleiben wollenden Leihgebern und im Besonderen der Familie von Helga Zahn | and all private lenders who prefer to remain anonymous and special thanks to the family of Helga Zahn.

Buch und Ausstellung entstanden mit Förderung durch | Book and exhibition are supported by
Christian-Heinrich-Sandler-Stiftung, Danner-Stiftung München, Kulturverein Schwarzenbach a. d. Saale e. V., Oberfrankenstiftung, Gemeinnützige Stiftung Sparkasse Hochfranken.
Besonderer Dank gilt der | special thanks to the Dr. Hans Vießmann-Stiftung.

KUNSTGALERIE ALTES RATHAUS
SCHWARZENBACH AN DER SAALE

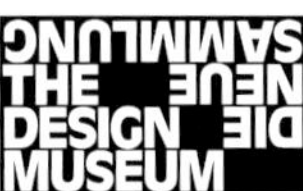

arnoldsche ART PUBLISHERS

ISBN-Nr. 978-3-89790-481-1

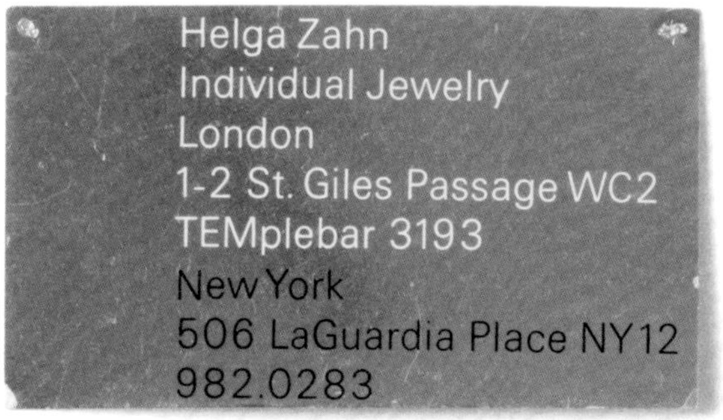

Helga Zahn
Individual Jewelry
London
1-2 St. Giles Passage WC2
TEMplebar 3193
New York
506 LaGuardia Place NY12
982.0283